Collins

EXPLORE ENGLISH

Student's Coursebook 3

William Collins' dream of knowledge for all began with the publication of his first book in 1819.
A self-educated mill worker, he not only enriched millions of lives, but also founded a flourishing publishing house. Today, staying true to this spirit, Collins books are packed with inspiration, innovation and practical expertise. They place you at the centre of a world of possibility and give you exactly what you need to explore it.

Collins. Freedom to teach.

An imprint of HarperCollinsPublishers
The News Building
1 London Bridge Street
London SE1 9GF

HarperCollinsPublishers
Macken House,
39/40 Mayor Street Upper,
Dublin 1, DO1 C9W8,
Ireland

> **Browse the complete Collins catalogue at www.collins.co.uk**

ISBN 978-0-00-836918-7

British Library Cataloguing in Publication Data

A catalogue record for this publication is available from the British Library.

Authors: Sandy Gibbs, Jennifer Martin
Series editor: Daphne Paizee
Publisher: Elaine Higgleton
Product manager: Lucy Cooper
Development editor: Cait Hawkins
Project manager: Lucy Hobbs
Proofreader: Helen King
Cover design by Gordon MacGilp
Cover artwork: Reprinted by permission of HarperCollins Publishers Ltd © 2010 (Steve Webb)
Typesetting by QBS Learning
Illustrations by QBS Learning
Production controller: Lyndsey Rogers

Printed and bound in the UK by Martins the Printers

Acknowledgements

The publishers gratefully acknowledge the permissions granted to reproduce copyright material in the book. Every effort has been made to contact the holders of copyright material, but if any have been inadvertently overlooked, the Publisher will be pleased to make the necessary arrangements at the first opportunity.

HarperCollinsPublishers Limited for extracts and artwork from:
Brown Bear and Wilbur Wolf by Sarah Parry, illustrated by Judy Musselle, text © 2012 Sarah Parry. *Too Hot to Stop!* by Stephen Webb, illustrated by Stephen Webb, text © 2010 Stephen Webb. *Let's Go To Mars!* by Janice Marriott, illustrated by Mark Ruffle, text © 2005 Janice Marriott. *Hector and the Cello* by Ros Asquith, illustrated by Ros Asquith, text © 2005 Ros Asquith. *The Brave Baby* by Malachy Doyle, illustrated by Richard Johnson, text © 2004 Malachy Doyle. *Hansel and Gretel* by Malachy Doyle, illustrated by Tim Archbold, text © 2006 Malachy Doyle. *Living Dinosaurs* by Jonathan Scott and Angela Scott, illustrated by Jonathan Scott and Angela Scott, text © 2007 Jonathan Scott and Angela Scott.

Photo acknowledgements

The publishers wish to thank the following for permission to reproduce photographs. Every effort has been made to trace copyright holders and to obtain their permission for the use of copyright materials. The publishers will gladly receive any information enabling them to rectify any error or omission at the first opportunity.

(t = top, c = centre, b = bottom, r = right, l = left)

p6t Nature Art/Shutterstock, p6tc Catmando/Shutterstock, p6c Aleksandar Grozdanovski, p6bc Eric Isselee/Shutterstock, p6bc Andrey Burmakin/Shutterstock, p17 Pyty/Shutterstock, p35l and r Jordi C/Shutterstock, p51 Maruricio Graiki/Shutterstock, p65tr Alexandr Junek Imaging/Shutterstock, p73b Corbis/Galen Rowell, p83 Macrovector/Shutterstock, p87 (mars) NASA/USGS, p87 (sun) NASA/SOHO, p95 Basheera Designs/Shutterstock, p119 (seasnake) poorbike/Shutterstock, p126 Jonathan and Angela Scott, p130 dioch/Shutterstock, p132 Vova Shevchuk/Shutterstock, p135t Grobler du Preez/Alamy, p137 aodaodaodaod/Shutterstock, p143 Monkey Business Images/Shutterstock, p154 Duda Vasilii/Shutterstock

With thanks to the following teachers and schools for reviewing materials in development: Hawar International School; Melissa Brobst, International School of Budapest; Niki Tzorzis, Pascal Primary School Lemessos.

Contents

Unit 1 My world

Week 1 My family and friends

1   Fill in the information about yourself.

My name is _____.

My surname is _____.

I am _____ years old.

My home address is: _____

_____

_____

My favourite _____ is _____.

My favourite _____ is _____.

My favourite _____ is _____.

2   Answer the questions about the Chan family.

a) What job does King Fai Chan have?

He is a _____.

b) How old is Lee's sister?

She is _____ years old.

c) True or false?

Lee's sister is called Sandy. _____

Meg does not like swimming. _____

d) Who likes playing with his toes?

_____ likes playing with his toes.

3 Circle 'yes' or 'no'.

a) Chad is a boy.   yes   no

b) Marie is a boy.   yes   no

c) Chad is shorter than Marie.   yes   no

d) Marie is the youngest child.   yes   no

e) Sheena is taller than Nish.   yes   no

f) Chad is taller than Marie.   yes   no

g) Sheena is the tallest girl.   yes   no

h) Marie is the shortest child.   yes   no

Chad   Nish   Sheena   Marie

4 **Are you taller or shorter than your partner? Fill in the missing word and your partner's name.**

I am _____ than _____ .

5 **Fill in the information about your own family.**

_____ is the tallest person in my family.

_____ is the youngest person in my family.

6 **Draw a line to match each animal to a word that best describes it.**

a)

b)

c)

d)

e)

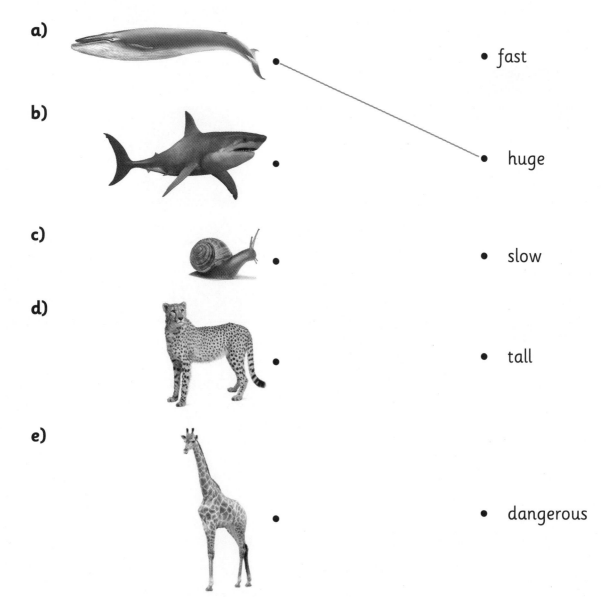

• fast

• huge

• slow

• tall

• dangerous

7 Animals have families too, and the members have different names. Complete the table. Use words from the box, and check in a dictionary if you need to.

| bull | chick | cub | doe | kitten | tom |

Animal	Mother	Father	Young
deer		stag	fawn
elephant	cow		calf
lion	lioness	lion	
chicken	hen	rooster	
cat	queen		

8 Fill in the missing words to compare the sizes of different animals.

a) A cub is small, a kitten is _____, but a chick is the _____.

b) A doe is big, a bear is _____, but a hippo is the _____.

c) A cat is strong, a lion is _____, but an elephant is the _____.

Week 2 My neighbourhood

1 **The pictures of the story are mixed up. Number them to show the correct order.**

☐  The town mouse knocked on the door.

☐  I'm going home where I can eat in peace.

☐  The town mouse invited the country mouse to join him.

☐  Watch out! There's a cat!

☐  The town mouse was so disappointed with the meal he was served.

☐  There was so much good food to eat!

2 **Do you think the country mouse will visit the town mouse again? Why?**

_____

3 **Think about this question.**

Imagine that you are the country mouse. The town mouse invites you for another meal. What will you say to him?

Week 3 My school

1 **Can you find these items hidden in the picture?**
   Circle each word as you find the item.

board	bookcase	computer	desk	dictionary
eraser	glue	keyboard	map	mouse	pen
pencil	ruler	scissors	sentence	teacher

I walk in the garden.

Diction

2 **Read the questions. Circle the correct words to complete the answers.**

a) Why did you eat the apple?

I ate the apple because I (was / is) hungry.

b) Why did you open the window?

I opened the window because I (feel / felt) too hot.

c) Why did Susie write a letter?

Susie wrote a letter because she (wanted / is wanting) to send her friend a message.

d) When did you begin your task?

I (begun / began) my task yesterday.

e) What did Jerry bring to school?

Jerry (brought / bringed) a ball to school.

f) What picture did Eli draw?

Eli (drew / drawed) a picture of a car.

g) Where did you find the books?

I (finded / found) the books in the small cupboard.

h) Did the teacher forgive the class?

Yes, the teacher (forgived / forgave) the class.

i) Where did Fadi go after school?

Fadi (went / goed) home after school.

j) Did Fadi pay for a new ruler?

Yes, Fadi (paid / payed) for a new ruler.

3 Look at the classroom on pages 8–9 in the Student's Resource Book. Fill in the correct number words.

I see _____ learners.

I see _____ teacher.

I see _____ boys.

4 Use the clues to complete the crossword puzzle.

Across

4 The leader of the school.

9 We use this to research the internet.

Down

1 We sit on this.

2 Your teacher writes on this.

3 One child, many _____.

5 We measure things with this.

6 We draw with this.

7 We use _____ to stick pictures in our notebooks.

8 We write with this.

Unit 2 Special days

Week 1 Traditions around the world

1   **Look at the picture. Complete the sentences with 'a' or 'an'.**

a)   I can see _____ dragon.

b)   I can see _____ envelope.

c)   I can see _____ lantern.

2   **Circle the correct word to complete the sentences.**

a)   The woman is holding (a / an) packet.

b)   She is pointing at (the / these) dancing dragon.

c)   (Those / An) boys are having fun.

d)   (This / These) is (a / an) exciting day!

e)   (That / Those) is (this / an) amazing sight.

f)   (A / The) Chinese New Year is (a / an) happy festival.

3   **Write three sentences about a special festival.**

1: _____

2: _____

3: _____

4 Choose words from the box to complete the sentences about Diwali.

> colourful   decorate   diyas   fireworks   gifts
> gold   houses   noises   petals   rangolis

Another tradition that is part of Diwali is the lighting of _____.

Diyas are oil lamps. People decorate their _____ with diyas

and other bright lights. This shows that evil is chased away from the

world. The world is no longer dark – it is filled with light.

During Diwali, people buy each other _____. Some people buy

clothes and others buy _____ jewellery.

During Diwali, people clean their houses and _____ the

courtyards, walls and entrances with _____ rangolis. The

_____ are made with coloured rice, dry flour, coloured sand or

even flower _____.

Diwali celebrations are not complete without _____. Hindus

believe that the loud _____ of the fireworks will scare away

evil from their homes.

5 Circle the correct word to complete the sentences.

a)

"Look! (Those / This) are pretty lanterns," exclaimed Biyu.

b)

"Is (those / this) lantern for sale?" asked Biyu.

c)

"How much does (that / the) one cost?" asked Biyu.

"(This / These) one costs more than the others," answered the man.

d)

"(Those / These) are my favourites," said Biyu happily.

6 **Read the poem about fireworks with a partner.**

BANG!

A ruby red star sparkles in the black sky

Up, up and up, higher than high,

A magical story, a very bright light

Come watch the fireworks with me tonight.

Brilliant blue bubbles, a shiny green glow

Fizzing explosions – Oh I love them so!

Just look at that rocket – see how it goes,

Where it will end up, nobody knows.

The fireworks float, they zoom and they blaze,

They make us so happy as upwards we gaze

Just look at the patterns that make the sky light –

We are so lucky to see them tonight!

by Jennifer Martin

7 **Read the poem again and answer these questions.**

a) True or false?

The fireworks sparkle in the sky. _____

The fireworks make patterns in the sky. _____

The writer knows the rocket will come back down again
near to them. _____

The writer thinks the fireworks are special. _____

The writer is frightened by the fireworks. _____

b) What colours are the different fireworks in the poem?

_____

c) How do we know the fireworks are being seen at night?

_____

_____

d) Complete these sentences.

I like fireworks because _____.

I don't like fireworks because _____.

I like fireworks, but _____.

I don't like fireworks, but _____.

e) Why do people have firework displays? List as many reasons as you can.

_____

_____

_____

_____

_____

8 Think about these questions.

Fireworks are used in celebrations all around the world.

Some people think fireworks are dangerous. Do you agree with this? Give reasons for your answers.

In some countries, fireworks may only be used in certain areas. Why do you think they have this rule?

9 **Find these countries in an atlas. Label them on the map.**

China

Egypt

Thailand

India

10 **Write a sentence about a festival celebrated in each country.**

China: _____

Egypt: _____

Thailand: _____

India: _____

11 Write the correct word under each picture.

| candle | diya | dragon | fireworks |
| lantern | krathong | rangoli | sunshine |

a)

_____

b)

_____

c)

_____

d)

_____

e)

_____

f)

_____

g)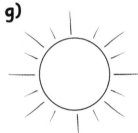

_____

h)

_____

12 Complete these sentences. Use words from activity 11.

a) _____ make loud noises and beautiful colours in the sky.

b) Families have a meal together in the _____.

c) Dancing _____ are made from silk, paper and bamboo.

d) A _____ is a small oil lamp used during Diwali.

13 Fill in the table.

Festival	Where?	What happens?	What do people do?
Chinese New Year			
Sham En-Nessim			
Loy Krathong			
Diwali			

Week 2 Fun times

1   **Complete this invitation for a party. Decorate the invitation to show the type of party you are having.**

Dear _____

You are invited to my _____ party!

Date: _____
Place: _____
Time: _____

Please let me know if you can make it.
From: _____

2 **Read the sentences. Are they facts, opinions or rules? Circle the correct word.**

a) Willem had a birthday party.   fact   opinion   rule

b) Willem had the best birthday party ever.   fact   opinion   rule

c) There was lots of food to eat.   fact   opinion   rule

d) It was the best party in the world.   fact   opinion   rule

e) Everybody must be polite at parties.   fact   opinion   rule

f) Parties with balloons are fun.   fact   opinion   rule

g) Boys do not enjoy parties.   fact   opinion   rule

h) You must say thank you after a party.   fact   opinion   rule

i) The children played games at the party.   fact   opinion   rule

j) The party ended after three hours.   fact   opinion   rule

3 **Look at the picture. Follow the instructions.**

Which cake has a candle on it? Circle it.

Which present is under the table? Colour it.

Find the balloon that is behind the table. Draw an X on it.

4 **Look at the pictures. Where is the cat? Write sentences using 'in', 'under' or 'in front of'.**

5 Cross out the incorrect word in each sentence.

a) Willem has (many / any) friends.

b) He had (a lot / no) of fun at his party.

c) The children played (some / no) games and their favourite was *Pass the parcel*.

d) There were (some / a lot) snacks to eat.

e) (Many / Lot) balloons popped and made a big noise.

f) There were (no / any) costumes at the party.

g) Bonnie didn't know (any / a lot) people at the party.

6 Underline the correct sentence in each pair. Circle the incorrect word in the other sentence.

a) The present is in the table.

The present is on the table.

b) The balloon is in front of the present.

The balloon is on front of the present.

c) The girl is standing next of the cake.

The girl is standing next to the cake.

7 **Follow the instructions and add to these pictures.**

Draw a candle on the cake.

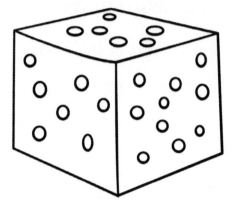

Draw a ribbon and a bow on the gift.

Draw two straws in the glass of juice.

Week 3 Party plans

1 **The pictures show which ingredients you need to bake a chocolate-chip birthday cake. Use the information to complete the list of ingredients.**

Ingredients for a chocolate-chip cake	Ingredients I need for two chocolate-chip cakes
_____ eggs	
1½ teaspoons of _____	
_____ chocolate-chips	
1 tablespoon of _____	
2 cups of _____	
1 cup of _____	
_____ of milk	

2 **Use the words from the box to complete the instructions for making the icing for the cake.**

| add | mix | pour | put | spread |

To make icing you will need:

- A mixing bowl
- A wooden spoon
- 1 cup of icing sugar
- 1 teaspoon of cocoa powder
- ½ cup of hot water
- Two cups of soft butter

Instructions:

First, _____ the icing sugar and cocoa powder into the mixing bowl.

Next, _____ the butter.

_____ in the hot water.

Then _____ the ingredients with the wooden spoon until you have a smooth paste.

Finally, _____ the icing evenly onto the cake.

3 **The instructions to make jelly boats are jumbled.**
Number them to show the correct order.

How to make jelly boats

[ ] Stir the mixture with a spoon until the jelly powder has dissolved.

[ ] Carefully scoop out the fruit. Place the fruit in a small dish. Do not break the skin of the orange.

[ ] Serve and enjoy!

[ ] When the jelly has set, decorate the orange boats with the flags.

[ ] Add the packet of jelly powder to the water.

[2] Boil some water.

[ ] Carefully pour the jelly liquid into the orange peel halves.

[ ] Place an orange on the chopping board. Cut it in half. Do this to all the oranges.

[ ] Gently put the orange peel halves into the fridge, for an hour.

[1] Wash your hands.

[ ] While the jelly sets, make small flags out of paper and toothpicks.

[3] Carefully pour 250 ml of boiling water into the mixing bowl.

4 **Circle the correct word or words to complete the sentences. The picture will help you.**

a) There are (any / many) eggs.

b) There is (a lot / not a lot) of milk left over.

c) There are (some / many) tablespoons.

d) There are (a lot of / not a lot of) eggs.

e) There is (some / no) milk.

5 **Write three sentences about the picture.**

1: _____

2: _____

3: _____

6 **Micah asked his friends what food they would like to eat at a party. Use the information he collected to answer the questions.**

	Snack 1: rotis	Snack 2: samosas	Snack 3: chocolate cake	Snack 4: ice cream
Children	7	4	11	12

a) How many children want to eat chocolate cake? _____

b) How many children want to eat samosas? _____

c) How many children want to eat rotis? _____

d) How many children want to eat ice cream? _____

e) Which snack would you choose? _____

7 **Draw a bar graph to show the information clearly.**

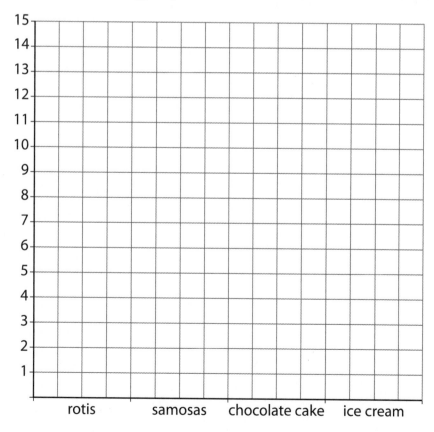

8   Circle the mistakes in this story.

Lucas was on a rush. He had to bake a cake, but he did not have enough ingredients. He went to the shop to buy what he needed.

Lucas put a bottle of milk around the basket. He also needed to buy flour and a butter. When he got home, he started to bake the cake.

First, he switched off the oven. Then he mixed the eggs, butter and sugar apart. Next, he added the milk or flour. He poured the batter on the baking tin and put it on the oven.

After 25 hours, Lucas carefully took the cake about the oven.

9   Rewrite the story correctly.

10 **Complete this table to plan a party for the twins, Kofi and Karl.**

Possible themes

Food and drink

Place

Games and activities

Decorations

Date and time

Clothing

Unit 3 Animal stories

Week 1 Helping baby elephants

1 Circle 'true' or 'false' and correct the false sentences.

a) Elephants eat plants.   true / false

_____

b) Elephants are brown and furry.   true / false

_____

c) Elephants have very small ears.   true / false

_____

d) Elephants are domestic animals.   true / false

_____

2 Match each word in the box to the correct meaning.

African elephant   bull   calf   cow   herd   ivory   orphan   trunk

Word	Meaning
	The name for an adult male elephant
	The name for a baby elephant.
	The name for an adult female elephant.
	Elephants with large ears found in Africa.
	A group of elephants.
	A young animal with no parents.
	Elephant tusks are made of this white material.
	An elephant's nose.

3 **Use the pictures on pages 16–17 in the Student's Resource Book to find the answers to these questions.**

a) What is the calf drinking?

_____

b) Who is the keeper feeding?

_____

c) What is on the keeper's head?

_____

d) What is the elephant eating?

_____

e) Who is looking after the elephants?

_____

4 **The answers to two questions about elephants are given. Write what the question could have been.**

They drink ten litres of milk a day for the first year of their lives.

At night they get looked after by their keepers.

5 **Unscramble the words to make sentences.**

a) ball. elephants the chasing The blue are

_____

b) milk. baby drinking is elephant The

_____

c) walking are The elephants slowly.

_____

d) baby lots fun. of elephants The are having

_____

e) calf. orphaned keeper feeding is the The elephant

_____

6 **Unscramble the letters to spell each word correctly.**

_____   _____   _____

epalhnet   eprkee   uktss

7 **Look at the pictures. Complete the two sentences about each picture.**

The elephant is _____.
The elephant likes to _____.

The elephant is _____.
The elephant likes to _____.

8 **Write your own sentences, using the words in the box.**

| ears | elephants | eyes | grass | trunk | ~~tusks~~ |

Example: _The adult elephant has large tusks._

_____
_____
_____
_____
_____

9 **Look at the pictures. Complete the sentences.**
Choose words from the box.

bath	drink	feed	play	sleep

a) The elephants like to _____ with the ball.

b) The thirsty elephant likes to _____ milk.

c) The elephants like to _____ in the mud.

d) The elephant wants to _____ because he is tired.

e) The keeper wants to _____ the hungry baby elephant.

10 **Listen and follow the instructions.**

Week 2 Swimming with dolphins

1   **Label the parts of the dolphin. Use the words from the box.**

| beak | blowhole | eye | fin | flipper | skin | tail |

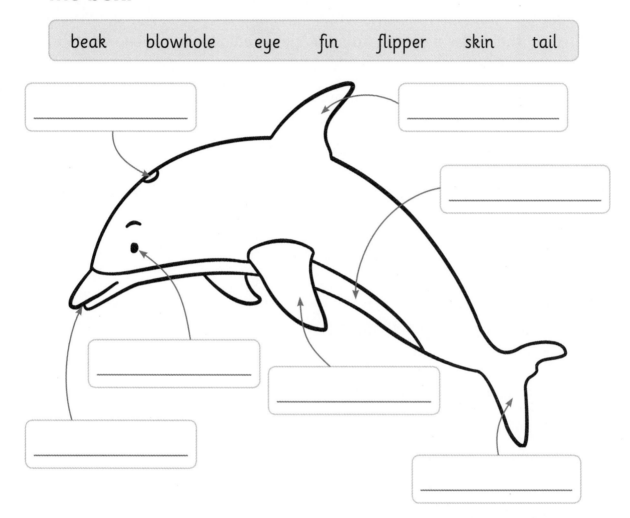

2   **Tick the words that describe the sounds a dolphin makes.**

☐ whistling   ☐ diving   ☐ squeaking

☐ clicking   ☐ rolling   ☐ calling

☐ roaring   ☐ beak   ☐ swimming

3 Circle the correct words in each sentence to complete the paragraphs.

When Mum (ask/ asked) me, "Do you want (to swim / swimming) with dolphins?" I couldn't stop (to smile / smiling). I often (see / am seeing) them in the water near my home in New Zealand and I love (watch / watching) them.

The dolphins (swam / are swimming) around me, leaping and playing. I (am diving / dived) deep but the dolphins (dived / are diving) deeper.

I (swam / swim) free, just like them!

4 Unscramble the sentences and rewrite them to match the story.

circled the sky. Sea birds in

_____

water. in splashed Something the

_____

put told wetsuit. She me to on a

_____

swam our towards boat. turned and The dolphins

_____

started feel I scared. bit a to

_____

5 Number the sentences in the correct order (1–5) to match the story.

☐ The dolphins swam around me, leaping and playing.

☐ Mum and I walked down the jetty to the boat.

38

	I raised my hand and returned to the boat. My dream had come true!
	Cathy showed me a poster of the types of dolphins we might see.
	"Dolphins," I called. "They're dolphins!"

6 **Circle the correct ending for each sentence.**

a) Dolphins live …   only in big lakes and rivers.
in oceans, seas and some rivers.

b) Dolphins use their blowhole for …   breathing.
hearing.

c) Dolphins communicate by …   hunting and eating.
whistling and clicking.

d) Dolphins eat …   fish, squid, shrimps and octopus.
sea birds, orcas and fins.

e) One way to protect dolphins is to …   not swim with them.
not put rubbish in the ocean.

f) When you swim with dolphins, …   you must have special equipment.
you wear boots.

g) Dolphins can swim …   backwards.
very fast.

7 **Write three new things that you have learned about dolphins.**

a) _____

b) _____

c) _____

8 **Complete these three sentences describing dolphins.**

1: Dolphins are _____

_____.

2: Dolphins have _____

_____.

3: Dolphins are able to _____

_____.

9 **Do you want to go swimming with dolphins? Circle 'want' or 'don't want' and complete the sentence.**

I (want / don't want) _____ to go swimming with dolphins because

_____

_____.

10 Match each question to the correct answer.

Where do they live? •

• Look after our seas and oceans. Don't put rubbish in the sea. Stop overfishing.

What do they eat? •

• Dolphins make whistling and clicking sounds, then wait to see if the sound bounces back off an object. Sometimes they slap their tails or touch each other.

How fast can they swim? •

• All over the world, in oceans and seas. Some even live in rivers.

How do they communicate? •

• A male dolphin can live for 25 to 30 years. A female can live for 50 years.

How long do they live? •

• They are carnivores. They hunt in groups to catch fish, squid, shrimps and octopus.

How can we help to protect dolphins? •

• Up to 40 km per hour.

11 Work with a partner. Look in some books or on the internet to find two new facts about dolphins. Write the facts here and share them with the class.

1: _____

_____

2: _____

_____

Week 3 Brown Bear and Wilbur Wolf

1 Write the missing letters in each word from the story. Then draw lines to match the words to the pictures.

a) b _ _ _

b) w _ l _

c) f _ _ h

d) b _ r _

e) b e _ _ e r

f) d _ _ r

2 Label the places shown in the picture. Choose words from the box.

| forest | meadow | mountain | river | valley |

3 **How is the character feeling in each picture? Choose words from the box.**

lonely	scared	strong	weak

a)

_____

b)

_____

c)

_____

d)

_____

4 **Write 'true' or 'false' next to each sentence.**

a) Brown Bear lost his sense of smell. _____

b) The birds, beaver and deer helped Brown Bear to catch food. _____

c) Brown Bear tried to eat the deer, the birds and the beaver. _____

d) Wilbur Wolf was too old and weak to catch food. _____

e) Brown Bear was hungry and lonely until he met Wilbur Wolf. _____

5 **Answer these questions with complete sentences.**

a) How do you help your friends? _____

_____

b) How do your friends help you? _____

_____

c) What did you like most about this story? _____

_____

6 **Think of words to complete the table. Use the example to help you.**

Characters	Words to show we don't like the character	Words to show that we don't mind the character	Words to show that we do like the character
Brown Bear	mean, sneaky	large, hairy	kind, brave
Wilbur Wolf			
The beaver			
The birds			
The deer			

Unit 4 Wings and things

Week 1 Birds

1 **Label the diagram. Choose words from the box.**

beak	claws	eyes	feathers	feet
head	legs	neck	tail	wings

2 **Match each bird to its name. Unscramble the letters and write the bird names.**

crow	hawk	heron	ostrich	parrot
peacock	puffin	seagull	woodpecker	

a)

triosch _____

b)

accekop _____

c)

roneh _____

d)

dopeowkcre _____

e)

wocr _____

f)

kwah _____

g)

tropar _____

h)

niffup _____

i)

glluesa _____

3 **Choose the three birds you like best. Complete the sentences.**

I like the _____ best.

I also like the _____ and the _____.

4 Answer these questions.

a) Which bird is the biggest? _____

b) Is a seagull bigger than a peacock? _____

c) Is a woodpecker bigger than a heron? _____

d) Is a puffin smaller than a heron? _____

e) Which bird is the smallest? _____

5 Read the sentences. Write 'true' or 'false'.

a) An ostrich can fly. _____

b) The ostrich is the biggest bird of all. _____

c) Some birds can learn to talk. _____

d) Woodpeckers eat things like crabs and prawns. _____

e) Owls can fly silently. _____

6 Complete the sentences below. Use the words from the box.

| bright | fruit | noisy | seeds | talk | tame |

a) The parrot is a _____ bird.

b) It has very _____ feathers.

c) Parrots can be taught to _____.

d) _____ parrots will not fly away.

e) Parrots eat _____ and _____.

7 Answer the question.

There are some goats and some birds in a field.
If there are 14 heads and 36 legs, how many birds
are there?

8 Circle the correct word in each sentence.

a) (A / An) owl catches a rat.

b) The (owl / owls) catch a mouse.

c) One (owl / owls) catches a mouse.

d) (A / Much) hawk swoops down.

e) (A lot of / An) hawks swoop down.

f) Many (hawk / hawks) swoop down.

g) (An / A) ostrich is a large bird.

h) (The / Many) ostrich is a large bird.

i) (Some / A) parrots made a noise.

j) (Much / Many) parrots make a lot of noise.

9 Read the information on pages 22–23 of the Student's Book again. Complete these fact files.

Seagulls	**Woodpeckers**
Description: _____	Description: _____
Where they live:_____	Where they live: _____
What they eat: _____	What they eat: _____
Ostriches	**Parrots**
Description: _____ _____	Description: _____ _____
Where they live: _____	Where they live: _____
What they eat: _____	What they eat: _____

10 **These are the first two pages of a book about birds. Read the information and answer the questions.**

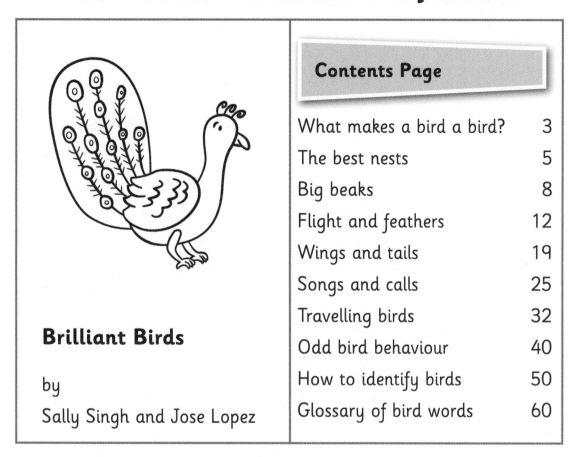

Brilliant Birds

by

Sally Singh and Jose Lopez

a) What is the name of the book? _____

b) Who wrote this book? _____

c) On which pages can you read about bird songs? _____

d) What can you read about on page 32? _____

e) Where would you look up the meaning of a word?

_____

f) How many pages have information about flight and feathers?

_____

g) Which chapter seems most interesting? Why? _____

Week 2 Fly like a bird

1 **Write the correct word next to each definition.**

| aeroplane | bellyflying | brave | dangerous | free fall | grip |
| parachute | safe | scared | skydiver | steer | team |

_____ A flying vehicle with wings and an engine.

_____ To control the direction in which something is moving.

_____ A person who jumps from a plane and falls to the ground before opening a parachute.

_____ The time before a skydiver opens his or her parachute when they are falling quickly through the air.

_____ Something that could hurt you.

_____ Holding onto other skydivers as you free fall.

_____ A group of people who do a sport or activity together.

_____ A special way of holding onto something.

_____ Not too scared to do something.

_____ Frightened or nervous about something.

_____ Equipment used in skydiving. This is a large canopy that opens and lets the skydiver fall slowly and safely to the ground.

_____ Something that won't hurt you or do any damage.

2 **Unscramble the letters and write the correct words.**

riskeydv

pleeranoa

ctuhepraa

_____   _____   _____

3 Complete these conversations with your own ideas.

a) Have you ever been to _____?

No, I have never _____ to _____, but I want to go there.

b) _____ you ever eaten _____?

No, I _____ never _____ _____, but I want to try it.

c) _____ you ever _____ a _____?

No, I _____ never _____ a _____, but I want to see one.

4 Listen to the interview with a skydiver. Fill in the missing words.

Interviewer: _____ you jump tomorrow?

Skydiver: Yes, I _____ definitely jump tomorrow.

Interviewer: What _____ you wear when you jump?

Skydiver: I _____ wear a parachute.

Interviewer: _____ you jump next week?

Skydiver: Yes, I _____.

Interviewer: _____ I come, too, and take some photos?

Skydiver: That's a good idea. _____ we jump together?

Interviewer: No thanks!

5 Circle five sports that you think are dangerous.

ice hockey
soccer
swimming
running

bowls
cricket
gymnastics
cycling

canoeing
mountain biking
bungee jumping
hang gliding

diving
hiking
horseback riding
kitesurfing

mountain climbing
skydiving
parkour
rock-climbing

roller skating
windsurfing
sailing
scuba diving

snorkeling
skateboarding
skiing
surfing

6 **Rank the sports you circled in activity 5, from the most dangerous to the least dangerous.**

Most dangerous: _____

_____

_____

_____

Least dangerous: _____

7 **Choose a sport from page 52. Write three instructions about how to do your sport.**

1: _____

2: _____

3: _____

8 **Write three things about your sport from activity 7. Use the words in the box.**

| a lot   always   never   sometimes |

Example: _You run a lot._

1: _____

2: _____

3: _____

9 Listen and follow the instructions.

a)	101	111
b)	1000	100
c)	900	999
d)	50	15
e)	880	800
f)	414	440

10 Use 'because' or 'but' to join each pair of sentences. Write the new sentences.

a) Joe tripped when he landed. He didn't hurt himself.

_____

b) Tina couldn't skydive. Tina was ill.

_____

c) We went on a plane. We wanted to skydive.

_____

d) I needed a different helmet. That one was too big.

_____

e) It was cold in the plane. We didn't notice.

_____

f) We couldn't see the ground. It was a cloudy day.

_____

g) I couldn't hold onto Joe's hand. I had the wrong grip.

_____

11 Read the poem.

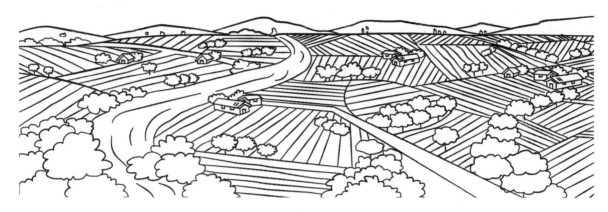

I Want to Be a Bird

I want to be a bird with wings
To fly around and see new things
Like little goats on mountains high
I'd touch the clouds as they float by.

I want to be a bird that soars
And doesn't live behind closed doors
Who flies around from here to there
Enjoying life without a care.

Imagine seeing the world from high –
My home is in the bright blue sky
What are those dots? Where are the farms?
Oh see those children waving their arms!

But oh dear me, I'll have to dive
Out of a plane – will I survive?
Indeed I will – count 1, 2, 3
I'm like a bird, I'm flying free!

by Jennifer Martin

12 Answer the questions about the poem.

a) Why does the poet want to be a bird?

b) Why do the farms look like dots?

c) What do these words mean?

float: _____

soars: _____

dive: _____

d) Is the poet really flying at the end of the poem? How do you know?

> 'Could' is the past tense form of 'can'.

13 Imagine that you jumped out of a plane with a parachute. What could you see and do? Write three sentences.

a) I could _____.

b) I could _____.

c) I _____.

> 'Must' means you don't have a choice to do something.
> You have to do it.

14 Write down three things that you 'must' do today.

a) I must _____.

b) I must _____.

c) I must _____.

Week 3 Fly facts

1 **Answer these questions about flies. Choose some of the words from the box.**

> a lot of   many   much   not many   one   six   ten   two

a) How many legs does a fly have?

A fly has _____ legs.

b) How many hairs are on a fly's legs?

There are _____ hairs on a fly's legs.

c) How many eggs does a fly lay?

A fly lays _____ eggs.

d) How many wings does a fly have?

A fly has _____ wings.

e) How many flies have you seen in your life?

I have seen _____ flies in my life.

f) How many different types of flies are there?

There are _____ different types of flies.

2 **Circle the correct word in each sentence.**

a) I am (chasing / chased) flies off my (food / germs).

b) I (must / could not) chase away flies to stop the spread of (food / germs).

c) Yesterday I (chased / chase) lots of flies off my table.

d) The rotten food (had / have) lots of flies on it.

e) Yesterday I (chased / am chasing) away flies because they are (dirty / clean).

3 Answer these questions as if you are a large housefly being interviewed.

a)

Why are your feet so dirty?

_____

_____

b)

Is it true that you spit on your food?

_____

_____

c)

What good things do you do?

_____

_____

d)

What are your favourite foods?

_____

_____

e)

Where do you live?

f)

Why do you rub your legs together all the time?

4 Tick the box that matches your opinion.

	Agree	Disagree	Don't know
Birds must not be kept in cages.			
Birds are better pets than cats.			
Birds make the best pets.			
You are sensible if you want to skydive.			
It's fun to jump out of aeroplanes.			
Skydiving is not dangerous.			
Flies are a nuisance.			
All flies must be destroyed.			
Flies make good pets			

5 **Unscramble the words to make sentences.**

a) must chase I flies away.

_____

b) I chased yesterday flies away lots of.

_____

6 **Choose the right words to complete the sentences.**

a) There is so (much / many) food and so (much / many) flies in the kitchen today. Please cover the food.

b) There is a fly sitting on that (lot of / piece of) meat!

c) Do you want to eat (many / some) food?

d) Flies carry (a lot of / much) germs.

e) There are (not much / not many) flies in winter, so we do not need to cover the food.

7 **Complete the story, using the words from the box.**

all	any	a lot	no	some

Once upon a time there was a fly. But this fly was not like

_____ its friends. It was a very strange fly because it did not

like germs.

It would not sit on _____ rotten food, even when it was hungry!

Even when there was _____ of old food on a plate or

_____ apples that were rotten, he preferred to sit on a clean

surface where there were _____ germs.

What a strange fly!

We use connectives such as *because*, *so* and *but* to link phrases. We use *because* to give a reason, *so* to give a result and *but* to contrast.

8 **Choose the best word to join each pair of sentences. Write the new sentence.**

because   but   so

a) There were lots of flies.   We covered the food.

_____

b) We kept the window closed.   Some flies still got in.

_____

c) We couldn't eat the food.   It was covered with flies.

_____

d) Flies are pests.   Flies spread germs.

_____

e) Flies clean their legs.   Small pieces of food fall off.

_____

f) Flies don't have teeth.   They can't bite or chew.

_____

g) Most insects have four wings.   Flies only have two.

_____

9 Find the words from the box in the wordsearch and circle them. Then work with a partner. Take turns to test each other's spelling. Say a word from the box and check whether your partner can spell it.

~~dirty~~   germ   invisible   maggots   rotting   sticky   tiny   wings

i	n	v	i	s	i	b	l	e
d	u	c	n	t	i	n	y	s
i	a	l	g	g	e	r	m	t
r	c	e	w	i	n	g	s	i
t	i	v	l	e	h	i	i	c
y	m	a	g	g	o	t	s	k
e	t	r	y	p	c	t	t	y
r	o	t	t	i	n	g	s	r

_____   _____

_____   _____

_____   _____

_____   _____

Unit 5 Adventures in different places

Week 1 Too Hot to Stop!

1 **Find the words from the box in the wordsearch and circle them.**

back	begun	cool	me
parade	pool	shade	sun
	track	tree	

p	f	g	b	a	c	k	k	s	w
o	t	o	e	g	o	e	a	h	s
p	u	s	g	t	o	t	y	a	o
c	o	s	u	n	l	r	r	d	a
b	s	o	n	y	f	a	l	e	m
c	h	z	l	c	e	c	u	k	e
p	a	r	a	d	e	k	o	w	x

2 **The gazelle's name is Hoppitt because he hops and jumps around. Think of names for his friends. Write the names below each picture. Tell your group why you chose these names.**

Hoppitt _____ _____ _____

_____ _____ _____

3 **Number the sentences from 1 to 4 to match the order of the story.**

☐ "Stop it, Hoppitt, stop it," warned the falcon flying by.

☐ Hoppitt hopped over the sand dune and splashed into the desert pool.

☐ Hoppitt the Gazelle likes to hop, hop, hop!

☐ It was too hot for Hoppitt and his friends to stop.

4 **Look at the picture. Use words from the box to complete the sentences.**

> at   behind   between   in   into   next to
> on   opposite   over   towards   under

a) The sand cat is sitting _____ a cactus.

b) The fox is standing _____ the rocks.

c) The falcon is flying _____ the sand dunes.

d) The gazelle is jumping _____ the cool water.

e) The snake is slithering _____ the cool water.

f) The lizard is standing _____ the shade.

5   Read about sand cats. Answer the questions.

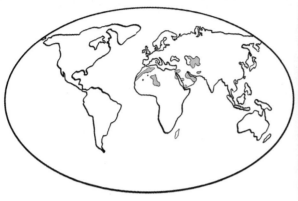 

The sand cat is a wild cat that is about the same size as a pet cat. Sand cats weigh about 3.4 kilograms. They look like pet cats but they behave and sound like wild cats.

The sand cat likes to live in the sandy desert. Its sand coloured coat makes it hard to see against the sand and dry bushes. It has thick fur on its paws so that it can walk on very hot sand without getting burned. It also has very big ears which help it hear very well.

The sand cat does not need to drink water to live. It gets almost all the water it needs from the animals that it kills and eats. The sand cat hunts animals to eat at night. It eats small animals like lizards and birds.

a)   Is a sand cat bigger or smaller than a pet cat?

_____

b)   How does a sand cat behave and sound?

_____

c)   Why is the sand cat difficult to see in the desert?

_____

d)   Why do you think it is called a 'sand cat'?

_____

e)   How is the sand cat well suited to living in the desert?

_____

6 **Use this table to help you make five sentences about the desert. Choose one part from each column to make each sentence.**

There is some	plants	near the rocks.
There are some	stones	in the desert.
There are many	trees	on the ground.
There isn't much	shade	growing there.
There aren't many	rain	to drink.
	water	under the bushes.
	animals	

1: _____

2: _____

3: _____

4: _____

5: _____

7 **Circle the words in each row that must be written with capital letters. Write the words correctly on the lines at the end of the rows.**

a) red   sahara desert   run   hurry   _____

b) jump   hoppitt   hot   snake   _____

c) middle east   shade   sand dune   sand   _____

d) africa   camel   lizard   parade   _____

8 **Rewrite each sentence correctly, using capital letters and full stops or question marks.**

a) have you seen hoppitt

_____

b) i saw him run past the lizard

_____

c) was hoppitt running very fast

_____

d) hoppitt was running as fast as the wind

_____

9 **Circle the best word to complete each sentence.**

a) The sand cat can live in a desert (but / because) it has adapted to the heat.

b) The sand cat doesn't need to drink water to live (because / and) it gets enough from the prey it eats.

c) The snake likes the heat, (but / so) it lies in the sun.

d) Hoppitt feels too hot, (so / because) he jumps into the cool water.

e) The falcon said 'stop it' (because / so) he could see a pool of water.

f) Hoppitt, sand cat, lizard (but / and) the camel were happy to jump into the water.

g) They jumped into the water (and / because) they felt too hot.

10 **Make up a good ending for each sentence.**

a) A fish likes water, but _a cat does not_.

b) A sand cat eats lizards because _____.

c) A camel can live in a desert because _____.

d) A snake slithers, but _____.

e) A falcon flies high in the sky because _____.

11 **What are the animals saying? Complete the conversation.**

Camel: It is so hot ...

Snake: I wish ...

Sand cat: I'm going to ...

Lizard: I'll just ...

12 **Name three animals that live in a desert.**

_____   _____   _____

13 **Circle the animal that does not fit in this group.**

cat   lion   tiger   bear

Why? _____

14 **Use these question words and make five questions that you could ask Hoppitt.**

a) Where _____?

b) How _____?

c) What _____?

d) Why _____?

e) Who _____?

Week 2 Racing in a city

1 What question was asked? Write in your ideas.

Question	Answer
	Rallying is a form of motorsport.
	It takes place on public and private roads.
	We're allowed to drive on both sides of the road.
	We must obey all the rules of the road on touring stages.
	The Dunlop Targa Rally of New Zealand is six days long.
	The co-driver must be good at navigation.

2 Complete the sentences, using the words from the box.

crew	co-driver	engine	helmet
route	rules	stage	support

a) The route is navigated by the _____.

b) The car is repaired by the _____.

c) The driver must start the _____.

d) They must obey the _____.

e) You must always wear a _____.

f) Tomorrow they will complete a _____.

g) That is a dangerous _____.

3 **Start at the star. Draw your own route on the grid. You may only move straight and turn left or right. Your route must end at the flag.**

Use a different colour to follow your partner's route.

4 **Complete the conversation below.**

Vince: The tyre is flat. Where is the jack?

Hans: I put _____ on the driver's seat.

Vince: Where _____is_____ the pump?

Hans: I left _____ in the support car.

Vince: Have you seen the co-driver yet?

Hans: Yes, I saw _____ with the driver. She was talking to him.

Vince: What did she say to _____?

Hans: She said _____ could still win the rally.

Vince: Do _____ think they can win?

Hans: I certainly do!

5 Read the clues. Complete the crossword puzzle.

Across

1 The car that comes first is the _____.

3 Part of a car that gives it power.

4 A part or section of a rally.

6 Direction or way to travel along a road.

7 A hard hat that protects your head.

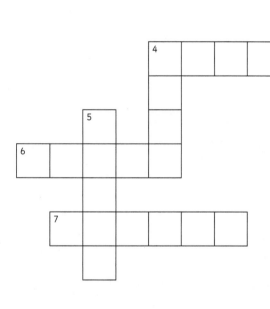

Down

2 Plan a route and follow it on a map.

4 Not in danger.

5 Instructions that tell us what we are and aren't allowed to do.

Week 3 In Antarctica

1 **Draw lines to match the words to their meanings.**

blubber •

pouch •

glaciers •

icebergs •

krill •

mammal •

orca •

• a flap of skin on a penguin's tummy which folds down over an egg, keeping it warm

• big pieces of ice floating in the sea

• tiny sea creatures that look like shrimps

• an animal that gives birth to live babies and feeds its young with milk from the mother's body

• rivers of ice that move very slowly downhill

• a layer of fat under the skin, which helps to keep some animals warm

• another name for a Killer whale

2 **Look at the picture. Label the animals and then answer the questions.**

a) How many seals can you see? _____

b) How many penguins are there? _____

c) How many orcas are jumping out of the water? _____

3 **Read the fact file to answer your teacher's questions.**

Fact file: Antarctic penguins				
Penguin		**Weight**	**Height**	**Food**
	Rockhopper	2–4 kg	45–55 cm	mostly krill
	Adelie	4–5 kg	70 cm	mostly krill
	Chinstrap	4–5 kg	70–75 cm	mostly krill
	Macaroni	5–6 kg	70 cm	mostly krill
	Gentoo	5–8 kg	75–90 cm	fish and krill
	King	10–20 kg	90 cm	fish and squid
	Emperor	20–40 kg	120 cm	fish and squid

4 **Write answers to the questions.**

a) Which penguin weighs the most? _____

b) What do most penguins eat? _____

c) Which penguin is between 70 and 75 cm high _____

5 **Which penguin do you think is the cutest? Why?** _____

_____

6 **Write down three questions to ask your partner.**

1: _____

2: _____

3: _____

Now answer your partner's questions.

7 Complete the sentences. Choose words from the box.

| coldest greatest larger larger smallest stronger windiest |

a) Antarctica is the _____ and _____ place on Earth.

b) The ocean around Antarctica has _____ waves and _____ winds than anywhere else on Earth.

c) Rockhoppers are the _____ penguins.

d) Seals are the penguins' _____ enemy.

e) King penguins are _____ than Adelie penguins.

8 Answer these questions.

a) Which penguins do not eat krill? _____

b) Is the King penguin taller or shorter than the Rockhopper penguin?

_____

c) How much do the heaviest penguins weigh? _____

d) Are you taller or shorter than a King penguin? _____

e) How much taller are King penguins than Macaroni penguins?

_____

f) Which penguins can weigh more than 10 kilograms? _____

9 Write the names of the different types of penguins in alphabetical order.

_____ _____ _____ _____

_____ _____ _____

10 Read the story about Herman the penguin chick's adventure.

Herman lived in Antarctica with his mother and his father. Herman's father, Mr King Penguin, loved swimming. In fact, he swam very well indeed! Mr King Penguin decided to go hunting for food, so he stopped talking to his friends and dived into the sea.

Mrs King Penguin was nowhere to be seen, so Herman decided to go and look for her. He hoped to find her quickly because he was feeling rather scared and lonely. "My mother likes eating squid. Perhaps she's in the water with my father," said Herman to himself. "I shall go and find them."

Herman jumped into the water. It was so cold, but he kept looking for his mother and father. He enjoyed swimming in the water, but he still wanted to find his parents, so he decided to go back home to see if they were there. "Oh Herman, we have been so worried about you!" said his mother. "You agreed to stay home all the time. Why did you go swimming without us?"

"I wanted to be with you. I'm sorry. I promise to always ask you first before I swim," said Herman.

11 Answer the questions about the story

a) What did Mr King Penguin do well?

_____

b) What did Mr King Penguin decide to do?

_____

c) Why did Herman decide to go swimming?

_____

d) Was this a good decision to make? Why?

_____

_____

12 **Unscramble the sentences to write five facts about seals. Remember to use capital letters in your sentences.**

a) six are there of seal kinds Antarctica. in

_____

b) kind of seal crabeater one the is seal.

_____

c) crabeater don't the crabs. seals eat

_____

d) eat they krill.

_____

e) icebergs. they on live

_____

13 **Write your own sentences about whales. Use each word in the box in its own sentence.**

biggest	orcas	krill	mammals

_____

_____

_____

_____

_____

_____

_____

14 Find and write the answers to these questions in your notebook.

a) Which ocean surrounds Antarctica?

b) Is Antarctica bigger than our country?

c) What is an iceberg?

d) Name one difference between Antarctica and the Arctic.

e) Name three different kinds of animals that live in Antarctica.

f) If you lived in the Antarctic, what would you rather have: a layer of blubber or a warm jacket? Why?

15 Write three reasons in each column.

I want to live in Antarctica because …	I don't want to live in Antarctica because …

16 **Fill in the missing words from the poem.**

Penguins are good at _____.

Penguins swim fast in the _____.

Penguins are good at _____.

I wish they'd come play with _____!

They love to _____ in cold water,

They _____ for krill and for fish,

They look after their _____ so carefully,

Oh, would someone please grant me my _____?

17 **Make up your own poem about whales. Use this writing frame to help you.**

Whales are good at _____.

Whales swim far out to _____.

Whales are _____.

I wish they would come play with me!

18 **Work in pairs to make up your own poem about seals. Your poem must have at least four lines and some words must rhyme. Write your poem on a sheet of paper and decorate it. Practise saying your poem aloud.**

Unit 6 Space

Week 1 The Solar System

1 **Read the sentences. Circle 'true' or 'false'.**

a)	Mercury is closer to the Sun than Earth is.	TRUE FALSE
b)	Venus has no atmosphere.	TRUE FALSE
c)	Pluto is a planet.	TRUE FALSE
d)	Mars is known as the 'Blue Planet'.	TRUE FALSE
e)	Jupiter is the largest planet in our Solar System.	TRUE FALSE
f)	Earth is the only planet that has a moon.	TRUE FALSE
g)	Saturn has rings and moons.	TRUE FALSE
h)	The Great Red Spot on Jupiter is a storm.	TRUE FALSE

2 **Choose the correct ending for each sentence. Write it on the line.**

a) We can't live on Jupiter because _____

it is very stormy.   it is too big.

b) We can't live on Venus because _____

it has an atmosphere of sulfuric acid.   it is too icy.

c) We can't live on Mercury because _____

it has no atmosphere.   it is too flat.

3 **Read the beginning of this sentence and think of a reason. Talk to your partner about it.**

Earth is a special planet in the Solar System because _____.

4 **Lena and Marco are talking about their project. Circle the correct words so their conversation makes sense.**

Lena: I am so excited. We are going to do (a / an) project on a planet. Let's do our project on Jupiter.

Marco: Do we have to do (the / that) project on Jupiter? Could we choose a different planet?

Lena: We could, but I have (many / some) information on Jupiter that we can use.

Marco: OK. Is (these / this) the information?

Lena: Yes, it is. Look! (This / Those) are pictures of Jupiter. Aren't they beautiful?

Marco: Yes, they are. I like (this / those) one more than (this / that) one.

Lena: Let's look for (some / many) more information.

Marco: I'll look through (the / these) books and you can look through (these / those).

Lena: I don't like (many / any) of the pictures in (these / this) book.

Marco: (Those / These) are good pictures here in (this / these) book. (That / This) is a good book to use.

Lena: Let's make a poster (about / from) Jupiter.

Marco: OK, let's do (that / those).

5 **Choose another planet. Write five facts about it.**

1: _____

2: _____

3: _____

4: _____

5: _____

6 **Work with a partner. Look at the picture. Ask each other questions about it.**

7 **Complete this list of questions to ask the aliens. Choose question words from the box. You may use the words more than once.**

How	How many	How much	What	Where

a) _____ is your name?

b) _____ old are you?

c) _____ do you live?

d) _____ times have you been to Earth?

e) _____ planets have you visited?

f) _____ do you travel through space?

g) _____ do you like to eat?

h) _____ do you come from?

i) _____ money does it cost to travel to your planet?

8 Play the 'Space Rocks' game.

You will need a spinner and a different coloured counter for each player.
Listen carefully to the rules of the game.

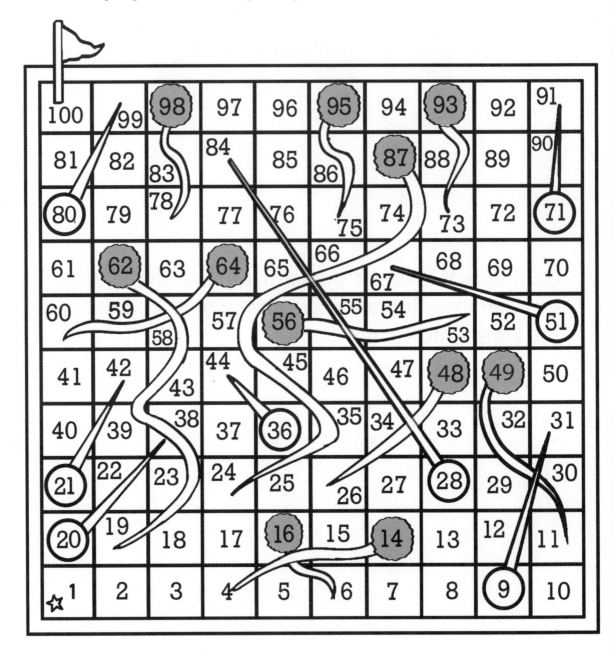

9 **a)** Label this diagram of the Solar System. Look at pages 34–35 of the Student's Resource Book if you need to.

b) Write one fact about Neptune.

_____

c) Write an opinion about travelling in space.

_____

_____

_____

_____

_____

_____

_____

10 **Complete the paragraphs. Choose words from the box.**

> aliens   asteroids   comets   meteorite   orbit
> Solar System   Sun   telescope   Voyager

Our _____ is made up of the Sun, planets and their moons.
The _____ is actually a star. Planets are not the only
things that move around our Sun. _____ are rocks that
_____ around the Sun, along with the planets. When an
asteroid falls to Earth, it is called a _____. It is a good
thing space is so big because _____ with tails of gas also
travel across the sky. They are small and icy, but their tails can be
very, very long!

Some stars are so far away from Earth that we need a
_____ to see them. Scientists sent a spacecraft called
_____ to take photographs and find out more information
about the planets. They found out a lot of new information about our
Solar System. I wonder what the _____ thought when they
saw a strange spacecraft flying through space?

11 **Try this word puzzle. Make a list of words with four or
more letters. Each letter may be used once per word.
Each word must have the letter E in it. Try to find at
least one word with nine letters.**

A	I	R
D	**E**	O
S	**S**	T

_____

_____

_____

12 Write a recipe for a delicious alien meal.

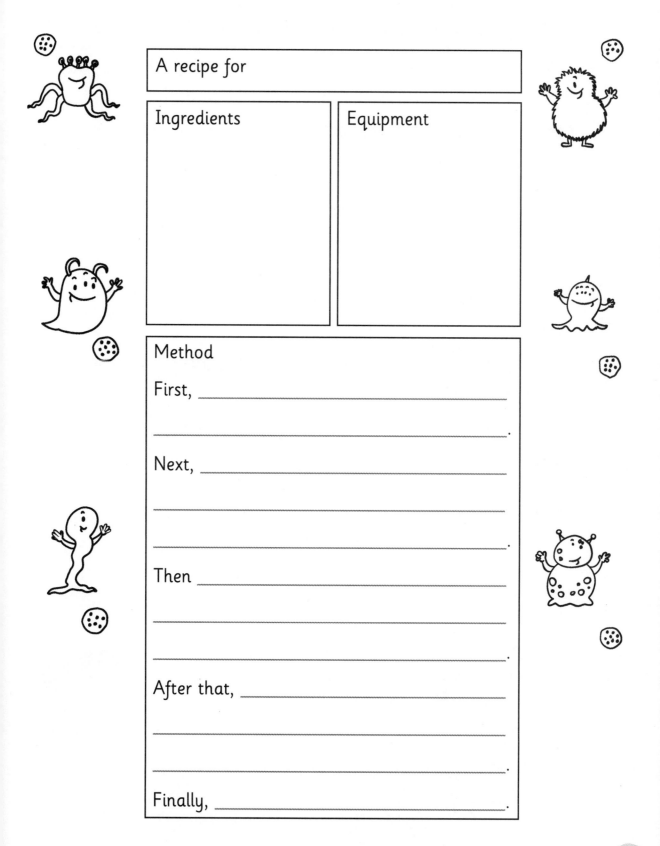

A recipe for _____

| Ingredients | Equipment |

Method

First, _____

_____ .

Next, _____

_____

_____ .

Then _____

_____

_____ .

After that, _____

_____

_____ .

Finally, _____ .

Week 2 Let's Go to Mars!

1 Read the questions and tick the correct answers.

a) How long does it take to get to Mars if you book tickets for the *Mars Express*?

three days ☐   three months ☐   three years ☐

b) What can hit your spaceship when it is in the air?

an alien ☐   a space junk ☐   another space ship ☐

c) What in-flight entertainment is there?

weightless football ☐   weightless tennis ☐

weightless swimming ☐

2 If people go to Mars, they might be able to phone people on Earth.

a) How long does it take for someone on Earth to hear you when you phone them from Mars?

b) These children are phoning their friends from Mars. Write what you think they are saying.

3 Look at the page and read the information about Mars.

4 Read what these children are saying. Tick the correct statements. Put a cross next to the incorrect statements.

- [ ] Mars is closer to the Sun than Earth.
- [ ] Mars is smaller than Earth.
- [ ] Mars is a ball of fire.
- [ ] Mars is much colder than your classroom.
- [ ] Mars is called the 'Blue Planet'.

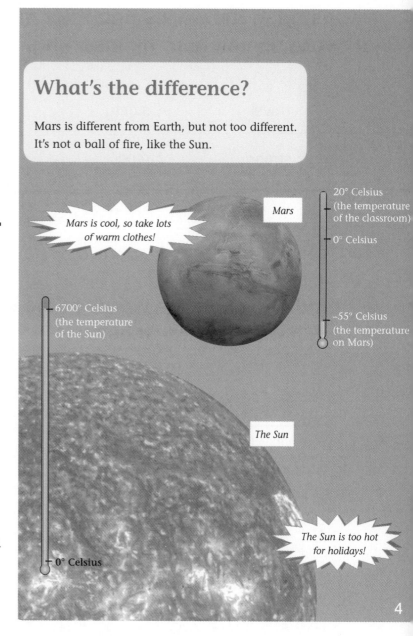

What's the difference?

Mars is different from Earth, but not too different. It's not a ball of fire, like the Sun.

Mars is cool, so take lots of warm clothes!

Mars

20° Celsius (the temperature of the classroom)

0° Celsius

-55° Celsius (the temperature on Mars)

6700° Celsius (the temperature of the Sun)

The Sun

The Sun is too hot for holidays!

0° Celsius

4

5 Write one true statement and one false statement of your own about Mars. Ask your partner to say which statement is false.

_____

_____

6 **Listen to the words and their meanings. Tick each word as you hear its meaning.**

☐	travel	☐	safety	☐	spaceship	☐	extra-light
☐	strong	☐	repair	☐	space junk	☐	entertainment
☐	weightless	☐	spacesuit	☐	outdoors	☐	orbit
☐	transfer	☐	parachute				

7 **Find and circle the words in the word search. As you find each word, rewrite it below.**

K	F	L	M	S	P	A	C	E	S	H	I	P
O	R	B	I	T	A	R	E	P	A	I	R	Q
P	W	G	S	A	F	E	T	Y	Z	H	R	S
A	C	W	E	I	G	H	T	L	E	S	S	P
R	I	E	X	T	R	A	L	I	G	H	T	A
A	S	P	A	C	E	J	U	N	K	S	G	C
C	T	R	A	N	S	F	E	R	T	S	U	E
H	X	N	P	Y	O	U	T	D	O	O	R	S
U	S	T	R	O	N	G	U	E	J	T	A	U
T	R	A	V	E	L	X	G	H	T	K	F	I
E	N	T	E	R	T	A	I	N	M	E	N	T

_____   _____   _____   _____

_____   _____   _____   _____

_____   _____   _____   _____

_____   _____

8   **Look at these diagrams. What do they tell you?**

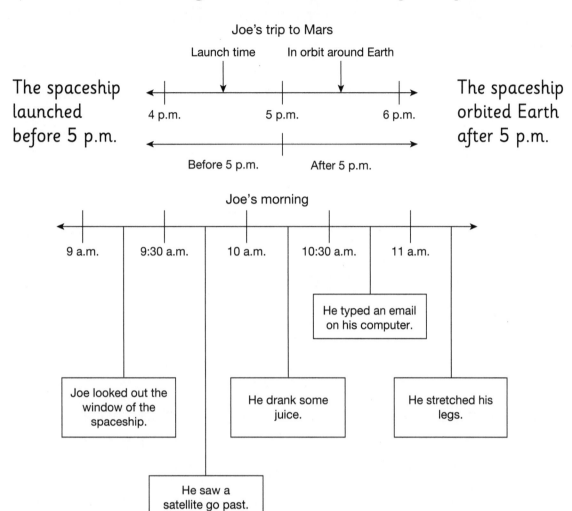

The spaceship launched before 5 p.m.

The spaceship orbited Earth after 5 p.m.

Joe's trip to Mars

Launch time   In orbit around Earth

4 p.m.   5 p.m.   6 p.m.

Before 5 p.m.   After 5 p.m.

Joe's morning

9 a.m.   9:30 a.m.   10 a.m.   10:30 a.m.   11 a.m.

He typed an email on his computer.

Joe looked out the window of the spaceship.

He drank some juice.

He stretched his legs.

He saw a satellite go past.

9   **Write two sentences about Joe's morning using the word 'before' and two sentences using the word 'after'.**

_____

_____

_____

_____

10 **Complete this letter from Fatima to her friend Rose, telling her about her trip to Mars. Use the words from the box.**

| best | colder | higher | largest | latest | longest |

Dear Rose,

I had a great trip to Mars. It was the _____ holiday of my life. It was also the _____ holiday of my life – nine months! I got to travel in comfort in the _____ spaceship! I saw the _____ volcano in the Solar System on Mars. It's three times _____ than Mount Everest! It was so much _____ on Mars than on Earth. I'm glad I had my warm spacesuit!

Your friend,

Fatima

11 **Imagine you are Joe from activity 8. You have just come back from your trip to Mars. Write a short email to a friend to tell them about it.**

```
 ○○○
 📄 📂 ◁ 📎 🗑
     To  _____
   From  _____
Subject  _____
```

Dear _____,

I'm just back from my very _____

The trip was so _____

The thing I liked most was _____

One thing that I really didn't like was _____

I am very glad that I _____

Your friend,

_____

12 Imagine you are going on a trip to Mars. Think about the things you will do there. Complete the answers to the questions.

Q: What will you do when you are there?

A: I plan to _____.

I also hope to _____.

I will try to _____.

Q: What will you enjoy doing?

A: I will enjoy _____ and _____.

13 We've given you some ideas of what you can do on Mars. Can you think of five new ideas? Write your answers in full sentences.

1: I can _____

2: _____

3: _____

4: _____

5: _____

14 Circle the correct words to complete the sentences.

a) Have you ever (being / been) to Space?

b) It is (exciting / excited) to go to Mars.

c) Ali is (dig / digging) a hole to look for water.

d) Have you ever (built / building) a sand yacht?

e) Do you (want / wanting) your photo taken?

f) We are (have / having) a sandcastle competition.

g) Have you ever (taking / taken) a selfie?

h) The wind is (blowing / blow) us all over the place.

15 Write sentences about the trip you took to Mars. Use the pictures to help you write about the things you could do when you were there. Start each sentence with 'I could …'.

_____

_____

_____

_____

_____

16 Answer the question.

It takes the astronauts five months to reach Mars. The spaceship they travel in is very cramped. They can't shower with water and only have tinned and freeze-dried food to eat. Do you want to travel to Mars? Why or why not?

Week 3 Believe it or not!

1 **What can you see in the picture? Tell your group.**

2 **Write five sentences about the picture. Use the words in the box to help you. You can use more than one of the words in each sentence.**

> and but craters Earth flag footprint
> moon landing Neil Armstrong or orbit
> oxygen planets spaceship spacesuit

1: _____

2: _____

3: _____

4: _____

5: _____

3 **Pretend that you are a newsreader. Read the story about the first Moon landing. Write 'has' or 'have' to complete the sentences.**

Men _____ walked on the Moon. The commander

_____ radioed to Earth. "Houston, Tranquility Base here.

The *Eagle* _____ landed," said Neil Armstrong.

The spacecraft _____ landed on the Moon. Neil Armstrong

_____ opened the hatch. He _____ planted the

first human footprint on the Moon. The crew _____

spent a total of two and a half hours on the Moon's surface.

The astronauts _____ become famous!

4 **Read the sentences. Underline the opinion sentences. Tick the fact sentences.**

☐ The Moon is not a planet.

☐ Earth is a planet.

☐ Earth is the best planet in the Solar System.

☐ Mercury is better than Venus.

☐ The winds on Mercury are stronger than the winds on Earth.

☐ It is good to explore space.

☐ Aliens will take over Earth!

5   **a) Look at the picture of Galileo standing next to his telescope. List ten words that describe him.**

_____
_____
_____
_____
_____
_____
_____
_____
_____
_____

b) Answer the question. Use some of the words from your list.

What was Galileo like?

I think he was _____

_____.

6 Use words from the box to complete these sentences.

Earth	house	ideas	moons
scientist	stars	Sun	telescope

a) Galileo was a _____.

b) He liked to study the _____.

c) Scientists believed that the Solar System moved around the _____.

d) Galileo believed that the Solar System moved around the _____.

e) Galileo invented the _____.

f) He discovered that Jupiter has four _____.

g) Many people were unhappy with his _____.

h) Galileo was not allowed to leave his _____.

7 **Choose an ending for each sentence from the box below. Copy the ending to complete the sentences.**

a) Galileo invented the telescope because _____

_____.

b) Galileo did not agree with some powerful people because _____

_____.

c) People argued with Galileo all the time because _____

_____.

d) Galileo was not allowed to leave his house because _____

_____.

e) Galileo was able to write about his discoveries, but _____

_____.

f) The powerful people decided that Galileo wasn't such a bad person and

_____.

> he said the planets moved around the Sun.
>
> he wanted to see things that were far away.
>
> they thought he was wrong.
>
> powerful people were not happy with him.
>
> later, he went blind and couldn't write any more.
>
> they were sorry for treating him so badly.

8 **Write three things you enjoy doing and three things you do well.**

I enjoy _____ , _____ and _____ .

I am good at _____ , _____ and _____ .

9 **Reesha and her friends have decided to build a spaceship. Read what they said and then answer the questions.**

I enjoy drawing but I hate finding things.

Reesha

I prefer finding things but I don't like painting.

Abdul

I like painting but I avoid building things.

Sita

I am happy building things but I don't enjoy drawing.

Verusha

a) Who will design the spaceship? Why? _____

_____

b) Who will find the parts for the spaceship? Why? _____

_____

c) Who will build the spaceship? Why? _____

_____

d) Who will decorate the spaceship? Why? _____

_____

10 **Use a pencil to mark all the missing punctuation marks and capital letters in these sentences. Then rewrite the sentences correctly.**

a) neil armstrong walked on the moon

_____

b) how many astronauts went to the moon

_____

c) what an exciting adventure

_____

d) the moon moves around earth

_____

11 **Look at some sentences from Neil Armstrong's diary. Circle the correct time words and phrases to complete the sentences.**

a) (Last year / Tomorrow) I trained to be an astronaut.

b) (Last week / Next year) I visited our space rocket.

c) (Tomorrow / Yesterday) we took off for the moon.

d) (Last week / Today) I am travelling through space.

e) (In ten years' time / Tomorrow), I will land on the moon.

f) (A month ago / Next week) I will be famous.

Unit 7 Story time

Week 1 Hector and the Cello

1   **Number the pictures from 1 to 5 to match the order of the story.**

2   **Fill in the missing words.**

   a) Hector decided he wanted to play the _____ .

   b) First, Hector spoke to the _____ .

   c) Next, he spoke to the _____ .

   d) Hector asked the lyrebird for _____ .

   e) Finally, all the animals played in an _____ .

3 Write 'T' for true or 'F' for false.

a) The lion wanted to play the cello. _____

b) Hector tramped through the desert. _____

c) The other animals weren't very kind to Hector. _____

d) Hector picked up the rhino's spots. _____

e) Hector found a cello teacher. _____

f) Hector learned to play the cello, but he wasn't very good. _____

g) At the concert, the animals were surprised and happy. _____

h) They all played music together at the end of the story. _____

4 Answer these questions about *Hector and the Cello*. Underline the correct answer.

1. Why did Hector tramp through the jungle?

   a) He wanted to make new friends.

   b) He wanted to find a cello teacher.

   c) He wanted to meet the lyrebird.

2. Which animal hissed so much she slithered out of her skin?

   a) the snake

   b) the lion

   c) the rhino

3. For how long did Hector have lessons before the grand concert?

   a) two weeks

   b) two months

   c) two years

4. How did the lyrebird help the other animals?

   a) The lyrebird gave them all a cello.

   b) The lyrebird sent them all back to where they came from.

   c) The lyrebird gave them back the things that they had lost.

5 **Look at the timeline of Hector's day. Write 'before' or 'after' to complete the sentences.**

sunrise → breakfast → lunch → tea → supper → sunset —two years→ concert

↓   ↓   ↓   ↓   ↓

Hector met the lion   Hector met the leopard   Hector met the rhino   Hector met the snake   Hector met the lyrebird

Example: Hector met the lion _after_ sunrise and _before_ breakfast.

a) Hector met the leopard _____ breakfast.

b) Hector met the rhino _____ lunch and _____ tea.

c) _____ supper, Hector met the snake.

d) Hector found a cello teacher _____ sunset.

e) _____ two years, Hector played his cello in a concert for the other animals.

6 **Fill in the missing words in the speech bubbles here and on the next page. Choose from 'that', 'this', 'these' and 'those' and 'is' or 'are'.**

a) _____ is my guitar.

b) _____ is his violin.

c) Are _____ our instruments? Yes, they _____.

d) Are _____ my drums? Yes, and they're very loud!

e) Is _____ a drum? Yes it _____ and it's big!

f) Are _____ trumpets? No they _____ not. _____ _____ flutes.

7 **Underline three sentences, to show the things you most hope to learn. Complete the last sentence, to show one more thing you hope to learn or do.**

I hope to play the cello.   I hope to play the drums.

I hope to sing in a band.   I hope to conduct an orchestra.

I hope to play the piano.   I hope to play the violin.

I hope to play the trumpet.   I hope to _____.

8 **Complete these sentences. Use words from the box.**

dark	dry	empty	fun	light	low	safe	wet

a) The jungle is too wet. Let's go where it's _____.

b) The desert is too dry. Let's go where it's _____.

c) The room is too dark. Let's go where it's _____.

d) The bridge is too high. Let's go where it's _____.

e) The room is too crowded. Let's go where it's _____.

f) This place is boring. Let's go somewhere _____.

g) The room is too light. Let's go somewhere _____.

h) The jungle is too scary. Let's go somewhere _____.

Week 2 The Brave Baby

1 **Write a label for each picture. Complete the sentences using some of your labels.**

a) The Chief spoke to the

_____ .

b) Wasso played with a

_____ .

c) Wasso lived in a

_____ .

d) The wise woman spoke to

_____ .

e) The Chief danced for

_____ .

2 **Write sentences to say what happened in the story in each picture. Write complete sentences. Use some of the words from the box.**

| afraid | blanket | brave | danced | fierce |
| laughed | sat | smiled | stick | |

_____

_____

_____

3 **Draw pictures to show the meaning of the words in the table.**

big	bigger	the biggest
small	smaller	the smallest
tall	taller	the tallest
fluffy	fluffier	the fluffiest
short	shorter	the shortest
happy	happier	the happiest

4 **Read and follow the instructions.**

a) Circle the tallest tree.

b) Colour the widest tree.

c) Draw an arrow to show the thinnest trunk.

d) Underline the narrowest tree.

e) Tick the fattest trunk.

f) Write labels for each row to compare the three trees in that row.
Choose a different thing to compare in each row.

5 **Use the words from the box to complete the sentences.**

| brave   tired   fierce   wise   special |

a) The _____ baby was not afraid of the chief.

b) The _____ Chief spoke to the old woman.

c) Wasso liked the _____ dance and she stopped crying.

d) The _____ Chief fell asleep.

e) The _____ woman was right.

6 **Match the beginning of each sentence with the correct ending.**

Wasso   •   • talked to the Chief.

All the people in the village •   • was a little baby.

The wise woman   •   • and fell asleep.

The Chief danced   •   • were scared of the Chief.

The Chief was tired   •   • and Wasso stopped crying.

7 **Write three sentences of your own about the story.**

_____

_____

_____

_____

8 **Are the following statements true? Write 'yes' or 'no'.**

a) The tents are near the trees. _____

b) The big tent is in front of the trees. _____

c) The women are looking inside the big tent. _____

9 **Write five sentences describing where different things are in this picture. Use the prepositions in the box.**

| at   above   below   behind |
| between   in   in front of |
| inside   near   next to   on |
| opposite   outside   to   under |

_____

_____

_____

_____

_____

10 **Look at the faces. Draw lines to match each face to a word that describes how the person is feeling.**

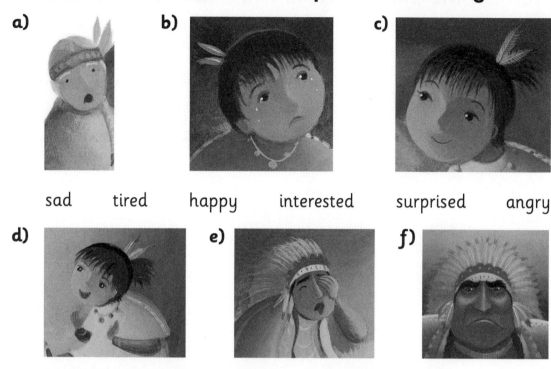

a)   b)   c)

sad   tired   happy   interested   surprised   angry

d)   e)   f)

11 **Read what the Chief wants someone to do.**

> I want the wise woman to fetch Wasso.
>
> I want Wasso to come to me.
>
> I want the villagers to dance with me.

a) What does the wise woman want? Complete these sentences.

I want the Chief to _____.

I want Wasso to _____.

I want the villagers to _____.

b) Write what you think these people are saying.

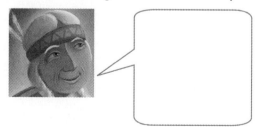

Week 3 Hansel and Gretel

1 **Number the pictures from 1 to 6 to match the order in the story.**

2 **Circle the correct word to complete the sentences:**

a) Hansel and Gretel went into the forest (with / by) their father.

b) They were left in the forest (by / from) their father.

c) They were lost, a long way (from / without) their home and (by / without) food.

d) They were invited into a cottage (from / by) an old woman.

e) They escaped (without / from) the cottage.

f) They were helped (by / with) an owl.

g) They lived happily ever after (with / by) their father.

3 Read the question. Tick the correct answer.

a) Who told the woodcutter to take Hansel and Gretel into the wood and leave them?

☐ the old woman   ☐ the stepmother   ☐ the woodcutter

b) Who dropped crumbs behind him as he followed his father?

☐ the woodcutter   ☐ Hansel   ☐ Gretel

c) Who wanted to eat the children?

☐ a wolf   ☐ the old woman   ☐ the stepmother

d) Who was happy the see the children return home?

☐ the woodcutter   ☐ the stepmother   ☐ the old woman

4 Put the words in the correct order to make questions. The answers have been given to you.

a) Question: What boy's was the name? _____

Answer: The boy's name was Hansel.

b) Question: children were How many there? _____

There were two children.

c) Question: Where go the children did? _____

Answer: The children went into the forest.

d) Question: Hansel leave Why did bread crumbs on path the?

_____

Answer: Hansel left bread crumbs on the path to help them get home.

e) Question: lived beautiful in the cottage Who?

_____

Answer: The old woman lived in the beautiful cottage.

5 **Write answers to the questions.**

6 **What will these children say if you ask "What's the matter?"**

7 Can you solve these riddles? Write your answers.

a) There are two of us. The woodcutter took us to the forest.

We are _____.

b) I am big and black. I am round and I get very hot.

I am a _____.

c) I fly silently. I can turn my head all the way round.

I am an _____.

d) I am a person. I cut wood.

I am the _____.

e) I am not young. I am not a man.

I am the _____.

f) We are small. We come from bread. Birds eat us.

We are _____.

8 Read the sentences. If the sentence is true, write 'T'. If the sentence is false, write 'F'.

a) The woodcutter took his children to the forest, because he was cross with them. _____

b) Gretel heard her father and stepmother talking. _____

c) The stepmother went with them. _____

d) The children saw the old woman's house in the morning. _____

e) The old woman was making a stew. _____

f) Hansel heard the old woman talking to herself. _____

g) An owl showed the children the way home. _____

h) The stepmother was very happy to see the children. _____

9 Write true sentences about each of these characters.

| Gretel | Hansel | old woman | stepmother | woodcutter |

10 **Write your own ending for each sentence.**

Hansel and Gretel's father is sad because _____ .

Their stepmother _____ .

Hansel dropped _____ .

These birds _____ .

This is where _____ .

The delicious house was _____ .

The old woman wanted _____ .

11 Help Hansel and Gretel get home.

Listen to the instructions. Play the game. The winner is the first person to reach home.

21	22 There's a tree in the path. Go back one block.	23	24	25 *Home at last!*
20 Stop for a drink. Miss a turn.	19	18 Get stuck in some mud. Go down one block.	17	16
11	12 You find a shortcut. Go up one block.	13	14 Your feet are sore. Miss a turn.	15 Build a bridge. Go up one block.
10 Stop! There's a river. Go back one block.	9	8	7 You find a clear path. Go forward four blocks.	6
1 *Start* →	2 Find a map. Go forward two blocks.	3	4	5 You hear a noise! Wait here until you spin a 2.

12 Think about the three stories in this unit.

a) Tick boxes to show your opinion of each story.

b) Underline the name of the story you liked best.

Title	I didn't enjoy the story	I enjoyed the story	I enjoyed the story very much!
Hector and the Cello			
The Brave Baby			
Hansel and Gretel			

13 Write a short review of the story you liked best. Use the writing frame below.

Title: _____

The story was about _____

_____.

The bit I liked most was when _____

_____.

My favourite character is _____ because

_____

_____

_____.

I liked this story the most because _____

_____

_____

_____

_____.

14 a) Find these words in the wordsearch. Tick the words as you find them.

☐ gingerbread ☐ stepmother ☐ forest ☐ stew

☐ Hansel ☐ Gretel ☐ hungry ☐ picnic

☐ owl ☐ path ☐ cauldron ☐ crumbs

g	i	n	g	e	r	b	r	e	a	d
n	f	o	r	e	s	t	e	k	o	r
j	s	t	e	w	e	f	f	y	w	p
l	r	t	t	h	a	n	s	e	l	i
m	p	x	e	c	r	u	m	b	s	c
c	a	u	l	d	r	o	n	s	g	n
s	t	e	p	m	o	t	h	e	r	i
r	h	u	n	g	r	y	d	n	b	c

b) Which two words are proper nouns? Write them here.

_____ _____

c) The meanings of some words are given. Write the word next to its meaning.

a large metal cooking pot: _____

a type of cake: _____

a bird with big eyes: _____

a place where there are lots of trees: _____

d) What do these words mean?

hungry: _____

crumbs: _____

Unit 8 Interesting animals

Week 1 Don't touch!

1   **Where do these animals live? Tick the correct columns in the table.**

Animal	In the sea	In fresh water	On land
penguin			
shark			
rabbit			
frog			
bear			
seagull			
jellyfish			
tortoise			

2   **Find all the sea animals in this picture. Draw lines to match the names to the animals.**

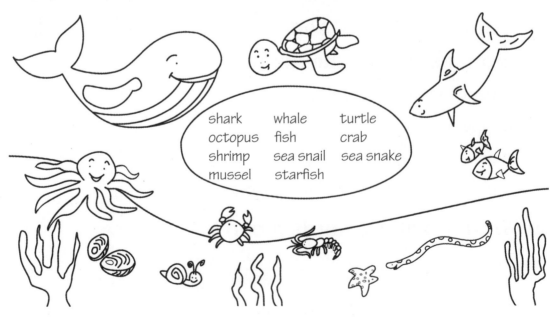

shark   whale   turtle
octopus   fish   crab
shrimp   sea snail   sea snake
mussel   starfish

3 What do you think? Tick your answer.

a) Which animal do you think is the strangest?

☐ porcupine fish   ☐ triggerfish   ☐ jellyfish

b) Which animal do you think is the most dangerous?

☐ electric ray   ☐ jellyfish   ☐ sea snake

c) Which animal do you think has the best camouflage?

☐ porcupine fish   ☐ sea snake   ☐ electric ray

d) Which animal do you think is scarier?

☐ electric ray   ☐ sea snake

4 Match the names to the animals.

jellyfish   porcupine fish   crab   sea snake   electric ray

a)   **b)**   **c)**   **d)**   **e)**

5 Which sea animals are these? Label them. Spell the words correctly.

a)   **b)**   **c)**   **d)**

_____   _____   _____   _____

6 Match the beginning of each sentence with its ending.

This triggerfish has   •   • because it is electric.

This crab has strong claws   •   • a sharp spine on its head.

This ray stays safe   •   • that cut and crush things.

The porcupine fish has spines   •   • their long tentacles that are poisonous.

These jellyfish can sting you with   •   • that can spike you.

7 Fill in the blanks with the correct word.

a) Sea animals look for _____ all the time.

(food / spines)

b) The crab has strong _____.

(claws / spines)

c) Some animals have found ways to stay _____.

(hungry / safe)

d) The triggerfish has a _____ on its head.

(spine / beak)

e) Jellyfish can sting you with their long _____.

(tentacles / beaks)

8 Read the sentences. Write 'true' or 'false'.

a) The jellyfish has a hard shell. _____

b) The crab has strong claws to cut and crush things. _____

c) The sea snake has fins. _____

d) The octopus has eight legs. _____

e) The shark has lots of big teeth. _____

9 **Read a learner's description of a shark. Write a short description of the other animals.**

A shark is a sea animal with dark grey skin. A shark has triangle-shaped fins and sharp teeth.		

10 **Choose words from the box to complete the sentences.**

strong claws	it is electric	a big spiky ball
ways to stay safe	spine on its head	

a) Sea animals have found _____.

b) The crab has _____ to cut and crush things.

c) The ray stays safe because _____.

d) The triggerfish has a _____.

e) The porcupine fish fills with water and looks like _____.

11 What do you want to be? Circle 'want' or 'don't want'. Give a reason why.

a) I (want / don't want) to be a shark because _____

_____.

b) I (want / don't want) to be a sea snake _____

_____.

c) I (want / don't want) to be an electric ray _____

_____.

d) I (want / don't want) to be a turtle _____

_____.

12 Choose the answer. Circle 'A' or 'B'.

a) Which animal fills with water when it feels threatened?

A   porcupine fish

B   triggerfish

b) Which animal has a hard shell?

A   starfish

B   sea snail

c) Which animal has strong claws?

A   shrimp

B   crab

d) Which animal has long tentacles that can sting?

A   jellyfish

B   turtle

e) Which fish has a spine on its head?

A   electric ray

B   triggerfish

13 **Complete the table to show how each animal protects itself. Tick the boxes.**

sea animal	spines	teeth	poison	claws	hiding
shark					
porcupine fish					
triggerfish					
crab					
sea snake					
jellyfish					

14 **Choose the animal from activity 13 you think has the best way to protect itself. Complete this sentence.**

I think the _____ protects itself best because

_____

_____.

15 **Circle the correct preposition to complete the sentences.**

a) The turtle is protected (by / with) a hard shell.

b) Shrimps are eaten (by / with) hungry fish.

c) The jellyfish can sting you (by / with) its long tentacles.

d) You mustn't get bitten (by / with) a sea snake - it's poisonous!

e) The porcupine fish fills itself (by / with) water.

f) The crab crushes things (by / with) its strong claws.

g) Lots of sea animals are hunted (by / with) sharks.

Week 2 Living dinosaurs

1 **Use the words from the box to label the parts of the crocodile.**

| eye | jaw | legs | skin | teeth | throat |

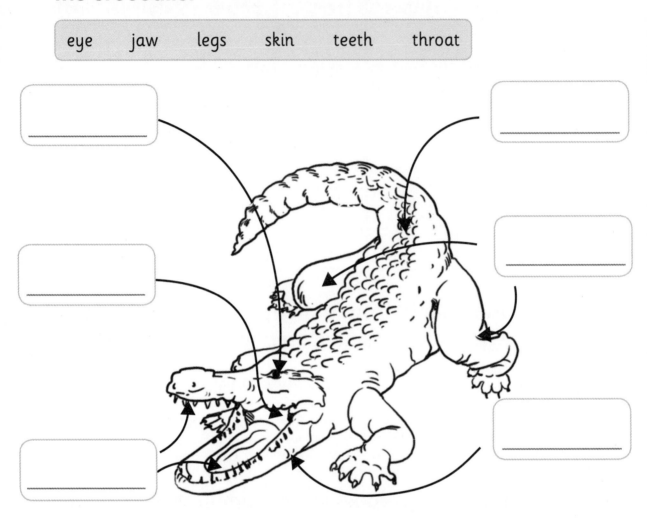

2 **Unscramble the letters. Write the words correctly.**

reprotda _____

sdraliz _____

noimtro rdzrila _____ _____

dicrescool _____

vgsecrsean _____

3 **Find and circle all the action words in the box.**

attack   crush   dragon   egg   eye   grab   hunt   jaw
legs   prey   skin   smash   swim   teeth   throat

We use the present simple tense to describe habits and things that are always true.

4 **Choose verbs from the box to describe the habits of crocodiles. Use the present simple tense.**

to be   to live   to sneak   to grab   to drown

Crocodiles _____ in and around water. They _____

very good hunters. A crocodile _____ up on its prey

and _____ it with powerful jaws. Then the crocodile

_____ the prey in the water.

5 **Complete the sentences, using the words in the box.**

to be   to catch   to drown   to eat

a) Crocodiles use their sharp teeth _____ and eat their prey.

b) Monitor lizards steal crocodile eggs _____.

c) Baby monitor lizards often live in trees _____ safe.

d) Crocodiles pull their prey underwater _____ it.

6 **Write a clear caption for each photograph.**

a)

_____

_____

_____

b)

_____

_____

_____

c)

_____

_____

_____

d)

_____

_____

_____

Pronouns

We use pronouns in the place of nouns because it is clumsy to repeat the nouns all the time. Pronouns can be the subject or the object in a sentence.

Subject pronouns: I you he she it we they

Object pronouns: me you him her it us them

7 **Replace the words in brackets with _her_, _it_ or _them_, without changing the meaning of the text. Use the example to help you.**

Female crocodiles lay their eggs on a sandy bank near the water, and they stay near their eggs to keep (the eggs) (1) _____them_____ safe until they hatch. This takes about 90 days. Both baby crocodiles and monitor lizards have a special egg tooth. They use (the egg tooth) (2) _____ to chip their way out of their eggs.

When the baby crocodiles are ready to hatch, they make a squeaky sound to warn their mother to take care of (the baby crocodiles) (3) _____. Next, the female crocodile carries (the baby crocodiles) (4) _____ in her mouth safely to the water.

Mother crocodiles look after their young and they will stay with (the mother) (5) _____ for about a year. She doesn't give (the baby crocodiles) (6) _____ food, however, and they need to find (the food) (7) _____ for themselves.

Baby monitor lizards are not so lucky! Like crocodiles, their mother doesn't find (the baby lizards) (8) _____ food, but, unlike crocodiles, their mother doesn't look after (the babies) (9) _____ at all. In fact, the babies never see (the mother) (10) _____ because she buries her eggs and then leaves (the eggs) (11) _____ before the babies hatch. Baby monitor lizards must be careful because other lizards like to eat (the baby lizards) (12)_____.

8 **The tables summarise the similarities and differences between crocodiles and monitor lizards.**

Crocodiles
live up to 80 years
up to seven metres long
have an egg tooth for chipping out of the egg
eat meat
eyes on top of their heads
powerful jaws and sharp teeth
look after their babies
powerful tail

Monitor lizards
live up to 40 years
up to three metres long
have an egg tooth for chipping out of the egg
eat meat
eyes on either side of their heads
powerful jaws and sharp teeth
do not look after their babies
powerful tail

To show differences, we can use the word 'but' in our sentences.

For example: Crocodiles can be seven metres long, but lizards are only three metres long.

To show similarities, we can use the word 'and'.

For example: Crocodiles eat meat, and so do lizards.

a) Write three sentences that show how crocodiles and monitor lizards are different. Use 'but' in each sentence.

1: _____

2: _____

3: _____

b) Write three sentences that show how crocodiles and monitor lizards are similar. Use 'and' in each sentence.

1: _____

2: _____

3: _____

9 **Look at this index page from a book. Answer the questions about it.**

INDEX

alligators 11
crocodile,
  babies 12, 13
  eggs 12, 13
  farming 11
  food 4, 5
  hunting 3, 6, 7, 8
  jaws 7, 10
  kinds 11
  size 9
  teeth 6, 9
  under water 8, 10

dinosaurs 2, 19
  egg tooth 18
Komodo dragon 14
monitor lizard,
  babies 18, 19
  food 16
  hunting 3, 15
  kinds 17
  size 14, 17

a) Can you read about the size of crocodiles on page 9?

_____

b) Can you read about different kinds of crocodiles on page 10?

_____

c) Can you read about monitor lizard babies on page 18?

_____

10 Look at the index page again and answer these questions.

a) What can you read about on page 3?

_____

b) What can you read about on page 13?

_____

c) What can you read about on page 6?

_____

11 What pages will you read to find the following information?

a) What is an alligator? _____

b) What is a Komodo dragon? _____

c) Where does a crocodile hunt? _____

d) Does a monitor lizard eat fish? _____

e) How many eggs does a crocodile lay? _____

f) Does a baby crocodile use an egg tooth to break its egg?

_____

g) What does a monitor lizard eat? _____

12 Choose words from the box to complete the information below. Then read it through to check you have chosen the correct words.

> crocodiles   dinosaurs   egg tooth   flap   lizards   monitor lizards
> powerful   predators   scavengers   sneaking   underwater

Did you know that crocodiles and lizards have been living on Earth for millions of years? These creatures were living at the same time as the _____. Dinosaurs are now extinct, but _____ and lizards are alive and well on our planet! We believe that they have survived for so long because they are such good hunters and

_____ .

Crocodiles catch their prey by _____ up on an animal. They drag their prey _____ to drown it. Have you wondered why the crocodile doesn't drown as well? There is a _____ of skin inside their throats that closes – just another reason why crocodiles have survived so long!

_____ _____ look a bit like crocodiles, but they are not related. In fact, the lizards try very hard to steal crocodile eggs to eat – they love eggs! Baby lizards use their special _____ _____ to crack their shells, but then they're on their own, as their parents do not look after them!

13 Skim read this information about monitor lizards to find information to complete the sentences.

Monitor lizards look a bit like crocodiles but they are not related. The largest monitor lizards in the world are the Komodo dragons. They can grow up to three metres long and live for 20 to 40 years. They like to hide and then rush at their prey and bite it with their powerful jaws. Their mouths contain poison, and even if their prey escapes, it often dies later from blood poisoning. Like crocodiles, monitor lizards are scavengers. They eat anything they can find. They eat fish, dead animals, birds, frogs and other small animals. But they especially like eggs. They dig out crocodile eggs from the nest and eat them when the mother crocodile is away.

a) Monitor lizards look like crocodiles, but _____

_____.

b) The largest lizards in the world are _____

_____.

c) The Komodo dragons bite their prey with _____

_____.

d) Their mouths are filled _____

_____.

e) If their prey escapes, it _____

_____.

f) Monitor lizards will eat _____

_____.

g) Monitor lizards eat crocodile eggs when _____

_____.

14 Write five full sentences about crocodiles. You can use information you already know or you can look up some new information.

1: _____

2: _____

3: _____

4: _____

5: _____

15 How do you feel about crocodiles? Write a full sentence giving your opinion.

_____

_____

16 Write five full sentences about monitor lizards. You can use information you already know or you can look up some new information.

1: _____

2: _____

3: _____

4: _____

5: _____

17 How do you feel about monitor lizards? Write a full sentence giving your opinion.

_____

_____

Week 3 Big, bigger, the biggest

1   **What do you know about Africa? Complete these activities before you start this unit.**

a) Look at the map of the continent of Africa. Answer the questions.

1: Which country looks the biggest on the map?

2: Which country looks the smallest on the map?

3: Is Morocco bigger or smaller than Egypt?

4: Which is bigger - Angola or Namibia?

5: Are there more countries that start with S or with M?

b) Work with a partner. Can you work out the quickest way to get from:

- Angola to South Africa?

- Sudan to Guinea?

- Mozambique to Morocco?

You can use words like these when you describe the way: *first, then, left, right, straight, up, down*

c) Tick the African animals in this list.

- [ ] rhino
- [ ] polar bear
- [ ] brown bear
- [ ] leopard
- [ ] lion
- [ ] walrus
- [ ] hippo
- [ ] kangaroo
- [ ] elephant
- [ ] tiger

2 **Circle the correct word in each statement. Use the pictures to help you.**

a) The elephant bull is (big / bigger / the biggest) animal in the picture.

b) The elephant calf is (small / smaller / the smallest) animal in the picture.

c) The elephant cow is (big / smaller / bigger) than the elephant bull.

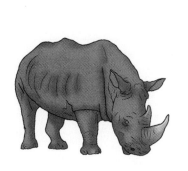  

d) Hippos are (smaller / smallest) than elephants, and live on the banks of rivers and lakes.

e) Rhinos are also (smaller / bigger) than elephants, but they can be as big as trucks.

f) Elephants are (bigger / the biggest) of the three animals.

3 **Label the diagram of the hippo. Use the words and phrases from the box.**

feet   four webbed toes   grey-blue skin   huge head
pink belly   short tail   two small eyes   two big nostrils
short legs   two small ears   very big mouth

4 Follow the instructions to write your own folktale.

Step 1: Choose your main character.

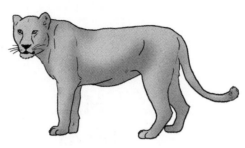

Step 2: Choose the setting for your story.

Step 3: Choose one of these problems for your story:

- Your character has lost something very special
- Your character is scared of his/her shadow
- Your character can't remember his/her name
- Your character is lonely and doesn't have any friends

Step 4: Brainstorm how to solve your character's problem. Write down your ideas. Then choose the best idea.

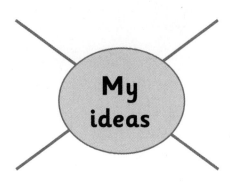

Step 5: Start your first draft using this frame.

Once upon a time, there was a _____ (main character) that lived _____ _____ (place). The _____ (main character) was very sad

because _____ _____ _____.

The _____ (main character) decided that he/she was going to solve his/her problem, so he/she _____ _____ _____ _____.

Step 6: Finish your story and tell it to a friend.

5 Read the information about rhinos. Highlight five important facts.

Rhinos (or rhinoceroses)

African rhinos have two horns on their noses. These are made of the same kind of material as our fingernails.

Rhinos have bad eyesight and they look clumsy. But few animals dare to attack them. They have excellent hearing and they can be bad-tempered.

A rhino can run faster than a human. It can also dodge and turn very quickly.

Rhinos live alone or in very small groups. They are fully grown at five to seven years old. They can live for up to 40 years.

There are two kinds of African rhino: the white rhino and the black rhino.

The white rhino isn't white at all. It has a wide upper lip, so the word 'white' should really be 'wide'.

Rhinos usually have one baby, called a calf. Rhino mothers look after their calves for several years.

6 Write 'true' or 'false'. Correct the false statements.

a) African rhinos have two horns. _____

b) Rhinos have very good eyesight. _____

c) Rhinos are friendly animals. _____

d) Rhinos can run fast. _____

e) The white rhino isn't actually white in colour. _____

f) The white rhino should be called the 'wide rhino'. _____

g) Rhinos make very good house pets. _____

7 Choose words from the box to complete the sentences. There are different ways of doing this.

good	better	the best
bad	worse	the worst
	more	the most
	less	the least

a) I think rhinos are _____ dangerous.

b) I think hippos are _____ dangerous than elephants.

c) I like elephants _____.

d) I like rhinos _____.

e) I think that poachers are _____ criminals.

8 Which wild animal do you like the most? Draw a picture of the animal. Write a sentence saying why you like it.

9 **Tick the boxes to summarise what you know about elephants, rhinos and hippos.**

facts	elephants	rhinos	hippos
An adult can weigh 6,300 kg.			
Live on the banks of rivers and lakes.			
Smaller than an elephant, but can be as big as a truck.			
People kill these animals for their tusks.			
People kill these animals for their horns.			
People kill these animals for meat and oil.			
Have bad eyesight.			
Have short legs and four webbed toes on each foot.			
Live alone or in small groups.			
Have a long trunk.			

10 Read the clues and complete the crossword.

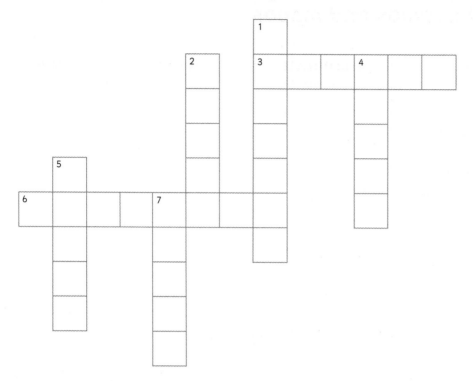

Across

3　The name of a continent where elephants live.

6　Game wardens protect elephants, rhinos and hippos from these people.

Down

1　Elephants, rhinos and hippos are three of the _____ animals on Earth.

2　Elephants, rhinos and hippos are called 'The Big _____'.

4　Poachers kill elephants for this.

5　A rhino can _____ and turn very quickly.

7　An African rhino has two of these on its nose.

Unit 9 Getting along

Week 1 We need friends

1 **What do friends do? Write four things that your friends do to make you feel happy.**

_____

_____

_____

_____

2 **Make a list of things you do with your friends and a list of things you do without your friends.**

Things I do with my friends:

_____

_____

_____

_____

Things I do without my friends:

_____

_____

_____

3 Draw a picture of one of the activities from activity 2 on page 143. Draw something you do with your friends or something you do without your friends.

This picture is by _____.

Tell a partner about your picture.

4 **Fill in the correct word to complete these sentences. Choose from 'by', 'with' or 'without'.**

a) My favourite song is _____ a band from Korea.

b) John walked _____ his brother to the park after school.

c) Ashraf was in trouble because he went to football practice _____ his P.E. kit.

d) There's a painting in the museum _____ Shereen's grandmother.

e) Anne went to school _____ her lunch today, but her friends shared their food _____ her.

f) He went to the museum _____ his class.

5 **Fill in the names of your friends in these speech bubbles to complete the sentences.**

a) My funniest friend is _____ .

b) My most helpful friend is _____ .

c) My cleverest friend is _____ .

d) My kindest friend is _____ .

e) My most talkative friend is _____ .

f) _____ is the best at sport.

g) _____ is the best at art.

6 **Now give reasons for your answers to activity 5.**

a) I think _____ is the funniest because _____ .

b) I think _____ is the _____ .

c) I think _____ .

d) _____ .

e) _____ .

f) _____ .

g) _____ .

7 **Write the correct words to complete the sentences.**

a) Laila checks her social media page _____ (a lot / never) because she wants to see what her friends are doing.

b) She _____ (a lot / never) goes to school at the weekend.

c) She _____ (often / always) catches the bus to school, but she _____ (never / sometimes) walks when the weather is nice.

d) She _____ (sometimes / always) buys lunch at school, but she takes her lunch box on a lot of days.

e) She _____ (always / never) brushes her teeth when she gets up in the morning and before she goes to bed.

f) Laila's birthday is _____ (always / sometimes) in June.

8 **Nina and Sally are from Egypt. Look at their school timetable, and then use the words from the box to complete the sentences.**

	Sunday	Monday	Tuesday	Wednesday	Thursday
1	maths	Arabic	science	sport	Arabic
2	English		maths	English	
3	science	social studies	Arabic		maths
	BREAK	BREAK	BREAK	BREAK	BREAK
4	sport	maths	English	maths	English
5			social studies	Arabic	science
6	Arabic	English	art		music
7				social studies	

at	after	before	in	on

a) It's Monday – Nina and Sally do English _____ maths.

b) It's Wednesday – they do sport _____ English.

c) Science classes are _____ Sunday, Tuesday and Thursday.

d) They do art _____ Tuesday.

e) It is Sunday, so sport is _____ the break.

f) Tomorrow is Friday and it is the weekend. They don't have lessons _____ the weekend.

g) After school, they do their homework _____ the evening.

9 **Listen to Nina talking about school, and complete the sentences.**

a) Nina and Sally's favourite lesson is _____.

b) Nina also likes doing _____.

c) Nina and Sally study science _____.

d) Sally enjoys doing _____.

e) They think _____ and _____ are interesting.

f) They spend time with their families at the _____.

Now read what Nina says and check your answers.

At school, I can spend time with my friend Sally. But we have to do lessons, too! Our favourite lesson is sport and we do this on Sunday and Wednesday. I like doing art, but we only do this on Tuesday. We always have Arabic, English and maths, and we also do science a lot. Sally enjoys doing music. We do this on Thursday, in our last lesson, before we go home.

In our break, we eat our food and love to sit and talk with our other friends about interesting things – like music and films.

Our weekend is on Friday and Saturday, when we spend time with our families.

10 **Make sentences with these words. Add capital letters, full stops and question marks.**

   a) his friends / on Mondays / he plays football / with /

   _____

   b) to / the swimming pool / tomorrow / shall we go

   _____

   c) on holiday / together / we will go / next week.

   _____

   d) my friends and I / a TV programme / six o'clock / watch /at

   _____

11 **Write a paragraph about what you do at school. Write about:**

   − **some of your lessons and when you do them**
   − **which lessons you like the most**
   − **things you enjoy doing with your friends.**

   _____

   _____

   _____

   _____

   _____

   _____

   _____

   _____

   _____

   _____

12 a) Read what Mara and Andi think about friends.

I think we all need friends. I see my friends every day because I feel lonely when I don't see them. We talk about everything. Sometimes we agree and sometimes we disagree, but we always discuss the things we are doing. That helps us to work out problems and to understand things. – Mara

I don't think you need to be with friends all the time. I know I like to spend some time alone. But it is good to do some things with friends. For example, on Fridays I go out with my friends. We talk about the week. – Andi

b) What do Mara and Andi think about friends? Underline four sentences that are true.

Mara thinks that friends always disagree.

Mara thinks that friends are important.

Mara thinks that friends can help you work out problems.

Andi thinks that you must go out with friends every day.

Andi thinks that we don't need to be with friends all the time to be happy.

Andi thinks that we need to spend some time with friends.

13 Circle the correct words to complete each sentence.

a) Next week I (will bake / will baking) cookies to thank my friends for their help.

b) (Will you to share / Will you share) your lunch with your friends today?

c) I (will always be kind / always being kind) to my friends because they help me.

d) (Will you always help / Will always you helping) your friends if they are in trouble?

e) What (you will do / will you do) next week with your friends?

Week 2 People who annoy us

1. **Read pages 61-62 of the Student's Resource Book. Are these sentences true or false?**

   a) Mark got the bus home from school.   True / False

   b) Mark was angry with the older boy.   True / False

   c) Mark planned to steal the older boy's school bag. True / False

   d) The sandwich had cheese and egg on it.   True / False

   e) Mark was smaller than the bully.   True / False

   f) He put chilli sauce on the sandwich.   True / False

   g) The teacher was angry with Mark.   True / False

2. **Read the story on pages 61–62 of the Student's Resource Book again. Then write a question to go with each answer.**

   a) What _____?

   Answer: The boy's name was Mark.

   b) When _____?

   Answer: The older boy took his lunch box at lunch time.

   c) How _____?

   Answer: Mark walked home from school.

   d) Why _____?

   Answer: Mark was angry because the older boy had taken his lunch again.

   e) Where _____?

   Answer: The teacher talked to Mark in her classroom.

3 **Find the words from the story 'Mark's Great Plan' in the wordsearch puzzle.**

brave bully chilli excited lunch mean older perfect
plan revenge sandwich school teacher understood

p	z	u	n	d	e	r	s	t	o	o	d	r	s	t
e	l	d	q	v	b	n	m	e	h	f	e	l	c	c
r	u	a	o	s	s	f	l	a	f	j	q	k	h	h
f	n	g	n	w	z	y	l	c	f	o	o	b	o	k
e	c	k	o	d	x	f	j	h	q	u	a	c	o	b
c	h	l	d	g	k	e	s	e	c	h	i	l	l	i
t	e	l	o	g	v	f	a	r	a	u	f	x	y	x
w	m	m	a	a	p	q	n	d	d	o	v	f	f	z
s	e	s	r	h	p	l	d	j	f	a	l	w	y	g
r	a	b	u	l	l	y	w	j	w	o	w	d	p	t
v	n	s	d	j	d	k	i	j	j	w	j	s	e	e
k	e	p	u	w	e	j	c	l	f	a	f	h	n	r
j	x	k	l	w	r	d	h	r	e	v	e	n	g	e
o	c	g	u	u	r	h	y	v	x	x	d	v	b	o
o	h	q	i	d	e	x	c	i	t	e	d	i	i	u

4 **Choose the correct word to make the second sentence mean the same as the first sentence.**

a) Mark put hot sauce in the sandwich.

He put hot sauce in (it / him).

b) The bully didn't like the sandwich.

He didn't like (it / him).

c) Mark was pleased with his plan.

He was pleased with (it / him).

d) The teacher talked to Mark.

She talked to (it / him)].

e) The teacher wasn't cross with Mark.

She wasn't cross with (him / it).

5 **Rewrite the sentences. Replace the underlined nouns with pronouns from the box. You can use the pronouns more than once.**

| him | her | it | them |

Mark made the sandwich for the bully.

Example: *Mark made it for him*.

a) Mark gave the sandwich to the bully.

_____

b) Mark told the teacher about the bully.

_____

c) The teacher spoke to Mark about his plan.

_____

d) The teacher told the learners to do their homework.

_____

6 Circle the correct word in each sentence.

a) The girl in the choir sings (beautiful / beautifully).

b) Sujin was (worried / worriedly) about the school test.

c) James ate his school lunch (hungrily / hungry).

d) The school band played (noisy / noisily).

e) The teacher was (madly / mad) at the student.

f) Lucy did her homework (sleep / sleepily).

g) Amy walked into the classroom (quietly / quiet) because she was late.

h) Mrs Gibbs was (angry / angrily) because the students wouldn't stop talking.

i) He is running (quick / quickly) because the school bell has rung.

j) The group of students did their school project (badly / bad).

7 Change the adjectives to adverbs and complete the sentences.

a) **neat**   Sara wrote her homework _____.

b) **worried**   We waited _____ for our quiz results.

c) **angry**   Our teacher shouted _____ because we wouldn't be quiet.

d) **slow**   My baby brother eats _____ because he is learning to use a spoon.

e) **happy**   The friends played _____ until it was time to go home.

8 **Draw lines to match the punctuation to its name.**

, •   • capital letter

. •   • full stop

Q •   • question mark

! •   • comma

? •   • exclamation mark

9 **Rewrite each sentence with the correct punctuation from activity 8.**

a) the older boy's name was peter

_____

b) stop it

_____

c) why do you always take my lunch

_____

d) mark made a sandwich with butter cheese tomato and chilli sauce

_____

e) go away

_____

f) the teacher was kind to mark

_____

10 **Imagine you are the characters in the story in the Student's Resource Book, Mark and Peter (the bully). Write a diary entry about what happened yesterday. Say how you felt.**

Mark's Diary

_____

_____

_____

Peter's Diary

_____

_____

_____

_____

_____

11 Choose words from the box to complete the sentences about Bella's busy week.

> evening   Friday   today   tomorrow   yesterday

What a busy week! _____ I went to the dentist. _____ I am going swimming in the afternoon. Then it is my dad's birthday party this _____. And then, _____, I will go to another party. It's my friend's birthday.

Next week is also very busy. I will go to my grandparents on _____, and then we are going away at the weekend!

12 Use adverbs from the box to complete the sentences.

> badly   carefully   kindly   slowly   suddenly

a) We walked home _____ because we weren't in a hurry.

b) Bullies are people who treat others _____.

c) The door opened _____ and my brother ran inside.

d) "Please run to the shop _____ and buy some milk," asked mum.

e) You must open the window _____ because it is windy.

f) He talked _____ to the new student.

13 Complete the sentences with 'from' or 'to'.

a) David walked from home _____ the party in ten minutes.

b) Sandy and Tobi walked home _____ school at 3 p.m.

c) Ranjit got a present _____ Dalia.

d) Molly walked _____ the museum to look at the pictures there.

Week 3 How to get along

1   **Look at the poster 'Bullies can hurt us in different ways' in the Student's Resource Book. Match these words to their meaning.**

meanest •   • make someone afraid

grab •   • hit hard

tease •   • say that you will hurt someone if they don't do what you want

threaten •   • make someone feel silly in front of other people

punch •   • the most unkind

scare •   • take something in a rough way

call someone •   • use descriptions that are not nice to make someone feel bad
  names

embarrass •   • laugh at someone to hurt them

2   **Unscramble the letters. Write the words about bullying correctly.**

ulbly   _____

craes   _____

neam   _____

npchu   _____

mberraas   _____

bakre   _____

3   **Choose three words from activity 2 and use them to write full sentences.**

1: _____

2: _____

3: _____

4 **Write what is happening in each picture. Use words from the box to help you.**

break   say mean things   tease   write mean things

a) _____

b) _____

c) _____

d) _____

5 Circle the correct word to complete the sentences.

a) He drew the picture (with / by) his best crayons.

b) My favourite book is *Paddington*. It is (with / by) an author called Michael Bond.

c) That painting on the wall is (by / with) Omar.

d) Dad made these pancakes (by /with) flour, eggs and milk.

e) I'm cleaning my hands (with /by) soap and water.

f) This song is (by /with) Ariana Grande. It's great!

6 A new student has just joined your class. Write five things that you can do to help them feel more comfortable and welcome.

1: I can _____

2: _____

3: _____

4: _____

5: _____

7 Work with a partner. Ask each other these questions.

a) What is the funniest thing you have done at school?

b) What was the most boring thing you did at school?

c) What was the most interesting thing you learned at school?

d) What was the nicest thing you have done for someone at school?

e) What was the best thing you have done for your friends?

8 **Give a new student in your class a list of instructions that will help them do well and enjoy school.**

Example: *Arrive before the bell*.

1: _____

2: _____

3: _____

4: _____

9 **Make questions with the words to match the answers given. Add capital letters and question marks.**

a) you / get along with / do / everyone / at school

_____

Answer: Yes. I get along with everyone at school.

b) walk away / did / he / when / the bully / he saw

_____

Answer: No. He didn't walk away when he saw the bully.

c) time / do you spend / how much / at the weekends / with your friends

_____

Answer: I spend a lot of time with my friends at the weekends.

d) jo and fred / where / go / after school / do / on tuesdays

_____

Answer: They go to the community centre down the road.